The Top Technologies Every Librarian Needs to Know

A LITA Guide

The Top Technologies Every Librarian Needs to Know

A LITA Guide

EDITED BY
KENNETH J. VARNUM

facet publishing

Published by Facet Publishing,
7 Ridgmount Street, London WC1E 7AE
www.facetpublishing.co.uk

Facet Publishing is wholly owned by CILIP: the Chartered Institute of
Library and Information Professionals.

First published in the USA by the American Library Association, 2014.
This UK edition 2014.

British Library Cataloguing in Publication Data
A catalogue record for this book is available from the British Library.

ISBN 978-1-78330-033-4

Printed and bound in the United Kingdom by Lightning Source.

Contents

Contents

Introduction

Everyone wants a crystal ball to help divine where to make investments in resources, technology, and time, so as to be better positioned to take advantage of whatever it is the future brings. Libraries are no different. This book was born of that desire, tempered by a dose of practical reality.

In a landscape where tools and trends change in a heartbeat, how can a library technologist know what has staying power and might well be the next big thing, worthy of serious attention? In this book, we have gathered experts on a range of emerging technologies to talk about just that. To avoid deus-ex-machina solutions to all our challenges, I asked the contributors to this book to stick to a near-term future, three to five years away—close enough to be in the realm of the predictable, but far enough away to ensure that the path to the future is not already paved.

Each chapter includes a thorough description of a particular technology: what it is, where it came from, and why it matters. We will look at early adopters or prototypes for the technology to see how it could be used more broadly. And then, having described a trajectory, we will paint a picture of how the library of the not-so-distant future could be changed by adopting and embracing that particular technology.

This is not a how-to manual for implementing the technologies, although there is some discussion about the hurdles that might need to be cleared to put each into place. Rather, the focus is on the impact the technology could have on staff, services, and patrons.

ABOUT TECHNOLOGY SELECTION

As you read this book, there are three basic things you should keep in mind as you develop a technology road map for your library's future: your library's longer-term goals, needs, and abilities. That is to say, you should look farther down the road than the current year's goals and projects, thinking more strategically. You probably are addressing the immediate needs of your library and patrons, or are working hard to do so. What you should be doing is looking farther down the road, seeking to discern what, broadly speaking, a successful version of your library will like.

Goals

The first area is strategic goals. There are many cool, interesting, and exciting technologies that your library could take on—we talk about many of them in this book. The foundation question to focus on, though, is where do you want to be? Technology cannot be the driver of your goals; it must be the enabling agent.

This preliminary question seems simple to answer but in reality is quite challenging. It requires an understanding of your community and where it is going. This is less an expression of what you must do than it is a matter of how you want your library to be characterized. At the same time, setting your library's goals is a much broader question than selecting technologies. The appropriate responses to your goals may have technological, organizational, and/or staffing answers. Without knowing what the targets are, an attempt to adopt a technology is likely to have, at best, a mixed result.

Depending on where your library is positioned in your larger organization, the degree to which you have autonomy over your own goals can vary. An excellent place to start, if you do not already have a set of strategic goals, is your parent organization's strategic plan. Where does it want to be? And how can you best position yourself to be in the right place?

Needs

Your future needs can be thought of in two parts. The first is related to what your library needs to do to meet the expectations of the community that pays your way (this might be your campus, your school, your community, or your organization). For some, meeting these needs might be the main contingency for continuing to receive funding. For others, meeting these needs is more intrinsic—the library doing its job well is sufficient justification on its own.

The second part of needs is related to what you require to continue delivering services in a cost-effective manner while remaining relevant to that community. The impact of free, always-on information services such as Google and Wikipedia should not drive library actions; but at the same time, offering something that those Internet sites do not is key to staying viable. This involves identifying the areas in which your library provides critical services to your community—access to licensed full text content, access to information technology, access to education, or whatever affordances you offer—and figuring out which are the ones you want to continue excelling at. If your library's future budget will be constrained, making a strategic decision to stop maintaining your own ILS could free up funds and staff to develop a digital repository for your community or to invest in digital versions of print materials. Knowing what the needs of community are will help guide you in making decisions to pursue one or another future technology.

Abilities

The third important factor to consider in positioning your library for new technologies is the abilities the people on your staff now have and the abilities you can reasonably acquire. Do you have the necessary staff to implement a new technology? What opportunities do you have to retrain existing staff to manage a new technology, or to acquire new staff to meet future needs? If you do not expect to be able to make significant staffing changes, then retraining becomes the obvious path. If you expect opportunities to hire new staff (either replacing vacant positions with different skill sets or adding new positions), that possibility opens new horizons for adopting radically different technologies than might otherwise be the case.

More broadly than staff abilities is the library's ability to take on new technologies or services. You could view this from a narrow view of capability—asking, "What skills do we have to bring to bear?"—but you can also think of this as constitutional capability. Is this a library whose culture readily adopts change or innovation? For example, if your library were to take the philosophically large step of moving to a cloud ILS system, would the people on your staff who are accustomed to near total control over the catalog's contents be able to make the switch?

MOVING FORWARD

These three areas of largely internal focus will help you determine where you want your library to be. Next is developing an understanding of technologies to help you get there. The rest of this book explores a range of technologies that have a high probability of being central to library services by the end of the current decade. Not all will be right for your library, depending on its size, purpose, and scope. But you will have a strong understanding of them and will be well positioned to make good judgments of which are right for you, and why they are—or are not—appropriate for you to adopt.

CONCLUDING THOUGHTS

Editing this book has been a challenging and exciting process. I have had the pleasure to collaborate with a talented and innovative group of authors. I thank them for their willingness to push the boundaries of their comfort zones as they wrote their chapters. I'm also grateful to Patrick Hogan, editor at ALA Editions, who was patient and flexible as this book evolved over several years. My appreciation also goes to Johanna Rosenbohm, who carefully edited the text and did wonders to clarify the unclarified.

Finally, I would like to dedicate this book to my two grade school–aged boys, Elliott and Milo. They will have the luxury of treating the technologies described here as commonplace. I cannot wait to see what technological marvels will strike *them* as innovative and exciting in the years to come.

Ken Varnum
Ann Arbor, Michigan
March 2014

Impetus to Innovate
Convergence and Library Trends

A. J. Million and Heather Lea Moulaison

The American Library Association (ALA) lists eleven core values of librarianship: access, confidentiality/privacy, democracy, diversity, education and lifelong learning, intellectual freedom, preservation, the public good, professionalism, service, and social responsibility.[1] In keeping with these values, especially the value of access, libraries historically prefer open-access solutions. In an industry white paper from 2013 surveying North American and European librarians on the topic of free online resources and access, the importance of open access was a predominant theme throughout.[2] Within this environment, information professionals seek high-quality content that will satisfy user needs. Yet, in the future, what trends will influence the use of technology in libraries? How will users expect to access content, and what will that content look like?

In this chapter, we look at library users for indicators of their current and future information-seeking behavior and their information-consumption patterns. We also consider the role of library acquisitions in light of the increasing importance of content as opposed to its carrier. In the following section, we examine and define the concepts of convergence and technological convergence, and what they mean to libraries in light of an emphasis on content and an increasing reliance on technology. Finally, we investigate how convergence is important to libraries now and how it will remain so in the future.

EVOLVING INFORMATION-SEEKING PARADIGMS

The needs and information-seeking practices of library patrons are presently evolving. Although power users of library systems will likely always be interested in the most powerful search options available,[3] not all information seekers require specific sources in order to meet their information needs. Users of information systems, including web users, often *satisfice,* the "information competency whereby individuals assess how much information is good enough to satisfy their information need."[4] "Good enough" represents a new paradigm in information seeking and requires information providers such as libraries to rethink the content they provide within the context of their stated values.

The amount of information available may not be the only negotiable aspect of information seeking given the information glut that Prabha et al. describe.[5] Particulars about the carrier, which we define as a content platform, may be less important than the access to the content itself. An e-book may be easier to browse for information on a device than a paper book, but a paper book will suffice in many instances. Blogs may contain content that is equally instructive, and Twitter may alert users to free online resources that further assist them in satisfying their information needs.

Differing carriers serve a purpose, but their content may well be complementary, cumulative, or potentially even interchangeable. In keeping with ALA's Core Values of Librarianship, by providing access to content, libraries may carry out their mission in today's complex information-rich environment. What can be called a format-agnostic focus on content is directly related to the concept of convergence, which may be briefly described as "the flow of content across multiple media platforms," and it is the primary direction in which the library of the future is moving.[6] Convergence will be discussed in greater detail in the next section.

One-Stop Shopping

In conjunction with the stated move toward carrier convergence, online shopping habits lend further insight into future user behaviors. Trends in online shopping seem to confirm that Web users are interested in one-stop shopping, the ability to learn one interface and to use it for multiple tasks. Amazon, the iTunes Store, Hulu, and Netflix all represent this model. Amazon has evolved since its inception to allow for the purchase not only of physical books and music, but also of groceries, electronics, and items that are difficult to find locally. The iTunes Store,

Hulu, and Netflix all offer electronic content in the form of music, movies, games, and television programs. Due to the nature of electronic media and sales, each of these online retailers can stock the widest range possible of content. There is truly something for everyone, as Chris Anderson describes in *The Long Tail*.[7]

As an example of the notion of something for everyone, we can point to heavy metal as a musical genre. Although brick-and-mortar stores might have a few selections in this category, online music retailers who only need to store the bits and bytes of an MP3 will likely have heavy metal, along with black metal, death metal, blackened death metal, brutal death metal, slam death metal, Swedish death metal (Swedeath), and sludge metal. Given the number of online customers, there will always be someone who will purchase songs in these categories despite their obscurity. The one-stop-shopping phenomenon has come to dominate the business models for online retailers of physical merchandise (e.g. Amazon), allowing for enormous stock, high turnover, and subsequently lower consumer prices.

To simplify their search experience, users often turn to one-stop shopping and prefer access to large collections. The discovery paradigm (dependent on relevance ranking) used in libraries presumes that library users also want a Google-like search box. With many formats and preferences in existence, the desire for simplicity and a universal collection is very strong; enough so, in fact, that one-stop shopping can also extend to physical service points (e.g., a circulation desk that functions as an information desk and assists with reference services).[8] Everything considered, the implication is that while patrons have carrier and content preferences, they ultimately put a premium on overall convenience. Large collections and effective search tools are one way of offering this.

Library Acquisitions

Libraries have sought to meet the expectations of patrons for years and will continue to do so well into the future. Presuming that a demand for the "Amazon" one-stop-shopping model extends to libraries, it remains to be seen how and if they can rise to the challenge; especially as adopting it requires the development of large collections of multiformat, digital material. Is a DVD copy of *Gone with the Wind* enough for users to satisfice, or should a library offer it on Blu-ray as well? If a library's music collection is small and on cassette tape, then will patrons abandon it and rely on commercial outlets and/or competitors instead?

Although the issue has yet to be resolved, a patron-driven acquisition (and thus access) model represents one way for libraries to carry out their missions. For electronic content, this approach has been remarked to be "a concept that easily and naturally moves beyond the print and media arenas into electronic books."[9] The point of interest here is not any particular technology or even recent investigations into the patron-driven acquisition model. Instead, given "shifts in the protocols by which we are producing and consuming media," patron-driven acquisitions offers a way for libraries to concurrently satisfice while asking users to select content in the format they prefer.[10] As media converges in the digital realm and can be used across multiple platforms, patrons expect access to comprehensive collections of material in their preferred format. Although many libraries cannot build one-stop-shopping repositories of a magnitude equal to Amazon, what matters is that libraries can still meet user expectations.

We have seen that libraries have strong values and well-defined missions that will continue to guide them well into the future. As patrons continue to change their search and information seeking behaviors, libraries will need to continue to meet their needs. Adaptable acquisitions policies are one way that this can happen. Next, we define the primary concept that will affect libraries, their acquisitions, and their approach to technology in the future: *convergence*.

CONVERGENCE TECHNOLOGIES

The general concept of convergence is identified by Jenkins in his book, *Convergence Culture*. In it, he states that

> ideas referenced by the term include the flow of content across multiple media platforms, the cooperation between multiple media industries, the search for new structures of media financing that fall at the interstices between old and new media, and the migratory behavior of media audiences who would go almost anywhere in search of the kind of entertainment experiences they want.[11]

Perhaps the most exciting aspect of a convergence culture is the use of technology to create, share, and access content that could not have otherwise existed. Convergence culture is notably participatory. For example, Jenkins explores the role of technology in the creation and dissemination of Harry Potter fan fiction among the community of young readers. Fan fiction is a kind of "grassroots creative expression" that flourishes when a variety of media and technologies are combined by members of a convergence culture to read, celebrate, compose, share, and consume.[12]

Applied to libraries and used by patrons, *convergence technologies* relate specifically to the multiplicity of platforms and formats (carriers) that can provide content. In the age of information overload, members of Jenkin's convergence culture (e.g., library patrons) cherry-pick content, satisficing as necessary and using one-stop-shopping strategies that are able to meet their information needs. Often, the use of technology plays a leading role in their practices as well. Continuing further, the definition of "convergence technologies" in *Technologies of Freedom* is those technologies that blur:

> the lines between media, even between point-to-point communications, such as the post, telephone and telegraph, and mass communication, such as the press, radio, and television.[13]

In regards to libraries, we identify *convergence* as the coming together of analog and digital formats in the form of 1s and 0s on digital computers, which may be transmitted electronically online, on air, or by any other form of communication. However, far from being a purely technology-driven phenomenon, the process of convergence also influences culture and patron behavior as well. Since this is the case, the terms *convergence* and *convergence technologies* can be used to not only describe digitization but also its cultural impact.

In the realm of convergence culture, technology is nonetheless a means to an end. The definition of technology is a broad and inclusive one, going beyond the notion of new and emerging technologies to embrace any human-made instrument used, in this case, for communication. Technology for technology's sake is never a winning strategy, as technology is simply an instrument to support use. Use, ultimately, is the aspect of activity that matters. Fan fiction is the quintessential creative outlet for some, but others in search of a creative outlet may equally wish to make a video, attend a book club session, or participate in community theater. The need is not for the technology per se, but for the outlet. Libraries have a tradition and a mission of providing both, and in the future, they may see their work converge just as technologies are converging at present.

5

CONVERGENCE TECHNOLOGIES IN LIBRARIES

Given their ubiquity, convergence technologies have found their way into libraries through the many materials that libraries collect and maintain and the events that they host. One obvious instance of convergence is the acquisition of analog media and digital media: format-agnostic patrons may not be concerned about checking out a print book instead of an e-book, or vice versa. MP4 in lieu of a DVD might be just fine for many.

Other issues of convergence might be less obvious. Does an online community bulletin board have the exact same function as the physical one? What about virtual reference books as compared to physical ones? Other questions of convergence strike more closely to the mission of the library. For example, do social tags left by patrons in LibraryThing count as an electronic version of what normally is professional reader's advisory if the patron ends up discovering a book she enjoys?

The question of obsolete technologies also plays a part. Patrons who can appreciate equally a vinyl record, an eight-track tape, a cassette tape, a CD, and an MP3 audio file are probably rare. Film, Betamax, VHS, DVD, Blu-ray, and MP4 video present a similar suite of format options that, though providing identical content, may not be able to meet the information needs of patrons. In the next section, we examine why convergence is the primary concept affecting future library technology trends.

Why Convergence Matters

The concept of convergence is essential to understanding the way content is consumed, accessed, and used both now and into the future. Thinking about the convergence culture is important to libraries in three ways: the technologies themselves, the systems used, and finally, the content that is offered. In this section, we will examine each in turn and provide insight into the future of convergence in libraries.

Limited Coexistence

For better or worse, a trend toward convergence sometimes brings competition. This can be problematic, given that the ability of libraries to build collections and provide one-stop-shopping access is often influenced by the unpredictable choices of the technology industry. Although coexistence, openness, and stability would be preferable, the reality is that considering the stakes involved with the adoption of shared media standards, cooperation between the giants in the technology sector is frequently undermined by competitive interests seeking to corner the market in their favor.

Several examples are worth noting here, especially Sony's Blu-ray and Toshiba's HD-DVD, as well as Apple's 2010 refusal to support Adobe Flash in its iOS platform. In the case of Blu-ray and HD-DVD, both were launched in 2006. Each sought to become a lucrative industry standard for high-definition optical discs.[14] Eventually the public adopted Blu-ray, and Sony reaped the benefits—but only after several libraries undoubtedly purchased HD-DVD collections. Steve Jobs's refusal to support Adobe Flash is another case in point; Apple prefers HTML5 as a standard on mobile devices.[15] Although Flash is not used to build collections of multimedia content, its obsolescence nonetheless indicates a broader trend showing how the interests of nonlibrarians cause some media formats to be adopted by the public while others are not.

Of course, competition extends beyond format standards too; companies and groups have competed to see their hardware or system become an adopted carrier for years. Just as groups often encourage their media format to become the convergent point of market standardization, the same occurs with electronic devices, especially computers. The famous longstanding feud between Apple and Microsoft serves as an example. Microsoft undercut Apple's superior operating system by selling DOS to IBM and the companies who copied IBM's architecture. For Microsoft, this was the serendipitous result of IBM's decision in the early 1980s to adopt open standards. Locked in by its own design, Apple was only able to sell its operating system to a limited number of retailers. The result was that Microsoft's market share grew and Apple's shrank. For the better part of twenty years, few consumers opted to buy anything but a PC.

How can libraries adapt if convergence encourages media companies to compete and create a never-ending stream of digital devices, formats, and standards? Is it possible to avoid turning a digital collection into a metaphorical library of babel? Fortunately, the answer seems to be that there are two solutions. First, competition sometimes results in a better product for both libraries and the public. As Microsoft and Netscape fought to see their respective browsers adopted in the late 1990s, some librarians took the opportunity to evaluate and select what was best for them.[16] Although competition may incentivize new standards, new products often are better than their predecessors. Second, while competition supercharged by convergence can force libraries to gamble on winners and losers, the nature of software, systems, and standards also provides a way forward. In some circumstances, open carrier and content standards represent a competitive advantage that aligns with the library community's preference for openness. Much like the case of Microsoft and IBM's computer standards, the result is that some business models favor stable standards that will not disappear. Libraries will certainly continue to focus on providing access to the content that patrons want and will continue to bet, using their best guesses, on the technology that will be the ones used by patrons according to the missions of their institutions. Open standards, however, ensure that this process is not as risky as it seems.

Library Systems

Convergence matters not only in the content and technologies that libraries offer, but also in the systems they use to offer files, media, or books. Traditionally libraries have used either vendor-supplied or in-house systems for both their electronic and analog content. With the advent of digital content and media, library technology has adapted, moving online and becoming increasingly sophisticated in the process. Discovery systems now provide seamless access to OPAC and licensed content as well as to locally created content held in institutional repositories and available over the Web.

Libraries have consistently opted to provide or promote creative and open solutions whenever possible. Content creation—including data, resources, metadata, and actual systems—has allowed and will continue to allow libraries to promote openness in providing access. Open-data repositories such as the University of Waterloo's Polar Data Catalogue (www.polardata.ca/whitesnow/) promote the exchange and use of geospatial data about the poles. Resources created by faculty, staff, and students are available in the University of Missouri's MOspace Respository (https://mospace.umsystem.edu) in a format that is OAI-PMH harvestable. Metadata about library materials, including "aboutness" and genre tags, can be crowdsourced in integrated library discovery systems, such as BiblioCommons, that supplement library metadata. Finally, libraries promoting the creation of new content though the use of makerspaces, do-it-yourself (DIY) workshops, and other community-involvement initiatives permit the creation of entirely new content in any number of formats to be delivered on any number of platforms or systems.

The continued adherence to open standards, no matter the system or environment, will also continue to serve libraries in the converged future. Linked data and the linked open-data movement provide for open standards that permit the use and reuse of data from a number of sources, including libraries. As libraries move to become key players in the linked data web,[17] their work provides the kind of structure needed for other linked data projects.[18]

Libraries have also promoted creative and open systems-based solutions to satisfy their own technology needs. Technology-centric library platforms have been growing and evolving since the 1960s when MARC (Machine-Readable Cataloging) was created at the Library of Congress. Proprietary and open-source integrated library systems (ILSs) coexist in the broader library ecosystem, and retrospective conversion and the addition of metadata assist with the organization, retrieval, and access to both analog and digital library content. The content of management systems and online, web-based systems complements the analog material housed in libraries. Digital content—licensed from vendors or procured by other means—does not replace but instead supplements the library's values of providing access. Drupal, WordPress, Omeka, and others are open-source software suites with robust library-user communities to support library access.

Having embraced convergence technologies by using creative, open solutions, libraries will continue to cultivate a culture of innovation. Specifically, libraries will adopt practical aspects of content management in new systems. This will assist them in carrying out the goal of providing access to library patrons and potentially encourage them to actively flag and/or identify new content for inclusion into a library according to a patron-driven acquisition model. It will also assist them in helping format-agnostic patrons, whose information seeking will continue to be challenged in a dynamic, competitive media environment.

Library Content

The final aspect of convergence worth discussing is how it impacts the way libraries offer access. After all, in the convergence culture model, the focus is on the mash-up, the creation of new content that could not exist previously. Convergence culture uses technology, but is above all participatory. This participatory component, a somewhat nontraditional approach, is one area in which libraries need to lead the way in providing a safe, reliable, neutral, and supportive environment for members of the convergence culture to go about creating, sharing, and accessing new content. Makerspaces in libraries are an excellent example of libraries promoting the creation of new content. Using a broad definition of technology, other examples may also be identified. Academic libraries that host technology workshops leading to the eventual creation of new content or software, public libraries that ask users to comment on novels in the online library catalog, archives that allow for patron interaction with manuscripts—all promote, potentially, a convergence of uses leading to the creation of new content.

One example of a public library planning to promote the creation of new content is the Woodneath Library Center's Story Center, outside of Kansas City, Missouri. The Mid-Continent Public Library's Woodneath Campus will feature:

- Collaboration and program space
- The Woodneath Press, an on-site bookmaking printer
- A digital storytelling technology lab
- A recording booth
- An archive of oral, written, and digital stories produced at the Center[19]

Library patrons will be able to work together collaboratively, much as the Harry Potter fan fiction writers were able to create, record, and share their own content. As content continues to converge across multiple platforms accessible in a variety of systems, libraries will want to be at the fore, offering resources for participating in the convergence culture that is being created.

A CULTURE OF CONVERGENCE

Library professionals are working in an era unlike any other, and the future promises to be even more exciting. A culture of convergence is driving the way that libraries collect and make information available to their patrons. Information is plentiful, but time and attention are scarce. Strategies that library users adopt in meeting their information needs include satisficing—choosing enough information and information that is good enough—from their preferred one-stop-shopping venue. In this time of technological convergence, libraries continue to be guided by values of providing access to quality content. But the carriers of that content will also change. The importance of access and of the content itself in the library context will persist, regardless of the formats or standards used. The systems that house library content will also continue to change and evolve as patrons' needs and tastes both change and grow. Finally, library content will increasingly reflect the format-agnostic reality of the convergence culture, focusing instead on the content that is relevant and of high quality.

Librarians must be prepared as we move into the future to continue to offer high-quality resources regardless of the platform or the format. When possible, they will favor open source solutions to meet patron needs. Above all, libraries will position themselves to be the platform that patrons use for the creation of and access to new content and will be a resource in the participatory culture that the convergence culture has enabled.

NOTES

1. American Library Association, *Core Values, Ethics, and Core Competencies,* January 27, 2009, www.ala.org/aboutala/governance/policymanual/updatedpolicymanual/section2/40corevalues.

2. Taylor & Francis Group, "Facilitating Access to Free Online Resources: Challenges and Opportunities for the Library Community" (white paper), May 2013, www.tandf.co.uk/libsite/pdf/TF-whitepaper-free-resources.pdf.

3. Thomas Mann, "Why LC Subject Headings Are More Important Than Ever," *American Libraries* 34, no. 9 (October 2003): 52–54; Thomas Mann, "The Changing Nature of the Catalog and Its Integration with Other Discovery Tools, Final Report: March 17, 2006, Prepared for the Library of Congress by Karen Calhoun: A Critical Review," *Journal of Library Metadata* 8, no. 2 (2008): 169–197, doi:10.1080/10911360802087374; Thomas Mann, "Will Google's Keyword Searching Eliminate the Need for LC Cataloging and Classification?" *Journal of Library Metadata* 8, no. 2 (2008): 159–168.

4. Chandra Prabha, Lynn Connaway, Lawrence Olszewski, and Lillie Jenkins, "What Is Enough? Satisficing Information Needs." Journal of Documentation 63 (1): 74–89.

5. Ibid.

6. Henry Jenkins, *Convergence Culture: Where Old and New Media Collide* (New York: New York University Press, 2006), 282.

7. Chris Anderson, *The Long Tail: Why the Future of Business Is Selling Less of More* (New York: Hyperion, 2008).

8. Janet Crane and Jeanne Pavy, "One-Stop Shopping: Merging Service Points in a University Library," *Public Services Quarterly* 4, no. 1 (2008): 29–45.

9. Judith Nixon, Robert Freeman, and Suzanne Ward, "Patron-Driven Acquisitions: An Introduction and Literature Review." *Collection Management* 35, no. 3 (2010): 119–24.

10. Jenkins, *Convergence Culture*, 14.

11. Ibid., 282.

12. Ibid., 191.

11

13. Ithil de Sola Pool, *Technologies of Freedom* (Cambridge, MA: Harvard University Press, 1983), 23, as cited in Jenkins, *Convergence Culture*, 10.

14. Will Smale, "How the PS3 Led Blu-ray's Triumph," *BBC News*, February 19, 2008, http://news.bbc.co.uk/2/hi/business/7252506.stm.

15. Steve Jobs, "Thoughts on Flash," *Hot News* (blog), April 2010, www.apple.com/hotnews/thoughts-on-flash.

16. Robb Waltner and Everett Algood, "Netscape vs. Internet Explorer," *The Serials Librarian* 36, nos. 1–2 (1999): 41.

17. For example, the Out of the Trenches project, www.canadiana.ca/en/pcdhn-lod.

18. See the work being undertaken at the Stanford Linked Data Project, http://lib.stanford.edu/stanford-linked-data-project/stanford-linked-data-project-0.

19. "The Future of Woodneath," Mid-Continent Public Library, accessed December 2013, www.mymcpl.org/woodneathplan.

Hands-Free Augmented Reality
Impacting the Library Future

Brigitte Bell and Terry Cottrell

BRIDGING THE GAP BETWEEN
THE PUBLIC MARKET AND LIBRARIES

The possible applications of augmented reality (AR) in the public consumer electronics market are virtually limitless. This chapter focuses on how these various applications translate to practical use within different types of libraries, from public to academic to small and large population–serving institutions. As can be seen with many other emerging forms of technology, market success in a broader cultural sense tends to be a harbinger for eventual widespread implementation within libraries. Library resources are becoming increasingly more mobile and increasingly more virtual; the next wave of library technology will likely build upon mobile applications made popular via handheld devices, with extensions of the same idea to newer, more innovative forms of delivery. This shift has been especially apparent in the evolution of augmented reality software.

OVERVIEW: AUGMENTED REALITY IN THE LIBRARY

Public Libraries

In the public library sphere, users vary the most in terms of access and ability to pragmatically integrate AR into their lives. Some public library patrons can willingly afford to purchase AR tools and technologies, and are simply looking for the addition of QR codes on shelves in key locations and perhaps a place to charge a device easily and conveniently. More and more airports today provide quick-charging stations for mobile devices, and more affluent library users will come to expect similar strategic convenience offerings in their library spaces as much as they have come to appreciate simple 110v outlets in cars, on trains, and in airport terminals. Other public library users have little to no idea that AR technologies exist, or that their libraries can introduce them to a new world of information that aims to use the physical world as a catalyst for the virtual. Why would these users, therefore, expect QR codes and other simple AR integration in their libraries? These individuals simply use the library for reading and the borrowing of movies, as they have for decades. With new AR integration in public libraries, these same users will come into their library for a familiar purpose and walk out with a new understanding of what can possibly be done with AR, because their library will lead them on the way to embracing this paradigm shift.

Indeed, while the variance of possibilities is infinite on the patron side within public libraries, the need to integrate AR into every public library is becoming more apparent and clear. A basic program for fast and nearly no-cost integration into small, medium, and large libraries is presented in table 2.1.

TABLE 2.1
Low/No-Cost AR Integration

Small Libraries
• QR codes at entrances and exits, and near special exhibits • Strong WiFi signal with unsecured access for ease of use and convenience • One person trained on staff to answer questions related to AR-capable mobile apps
Medium Libraries
• QR codes at all stacks describing basic contents • Multiple WiFi access point with encryption and security protocol within, and including external seating areas • Multipurpose open area/makerspace with projection capabilities for connection of user's own devices
Large Libraries
• Policy on use and local legal codes for wearable devices and image capturing within buildings • Active blog on AR apps and technologies with reviews from key staff • IT department trained to triage and assist patrons with mobile devices utilizing AR technologies • Multiple areas/makerspaces with projection equipment for utilizing library- and user-provided AR-capable devices • Training and demonstration schedule for AR technologies available for commercial, educational, and leisure purposes

While the aforementioned program can get most libraries into the business of providing basic AR services, it is advised that libraries of all sizes and types consider what policies and procedures from other like-sized institutions can be successfully gleaned and implemented at their own.

Academic Libraries

Most college students carry at least one mobile device that is capable of basic AR interaction.[1] As a result, some colleges and universities now look to use mobile technologies as the primary means of communication with their constituents, because students already have the communication tools with them each day.[2] Based on the high percentage of patrons using mobile devices, academic libraries' strategies for utilizing AR and serving the needs of these highly tech–equipped individuals are inherently different from that of public libraries. Academic library users will view many of the AR-related activities and offerings at their public libraries as more appropriate for their leisure time and activities. When they encounter AR at their university, they expect something different—AR that is discipline specific and research ready. The struggle for academic libraries is finding ways that the potential for leisure with AR can be swung toward assisting and facilitating research needs. It is helpful, therefore, to remember that college and university users come to their libraries both as individual researchers and also as individual members of scheduled courses. They use the library singularly for their own needs, but also jointly as groups in class settings. The former is where AR becomes much more viable for libraries of this type.

Insofar as AR is very helpful with finding desired locations (e.g., restaurants, clubs, parks, homes), it is inherently centered on discovery. This is where the tie to academic research begins. Academic libraries' focus on the need for faculty and students to "discover" information is how libraries can successfully form strategies for implementation. At this time, the focus of cutting-edge AR development is entertainment first, discovery second, and then training and education.[3] Research development on bringing AR into the sphere of online research content (i.e., online journals and video) is still in its infancy, with no clear company presenting a market-leading choice for university libraries. Academic libraries are wise to integrate QR codes and makerspaces in the same ways that have been mentioned before in public libraries, but always with the understanding that the raw amount of smartphones and tablets that college students carry requires libraries to standardize as much AR content development as possible on prevailing apps and devices. At this time, this leads academic libraries to Apple and Droid-based AR integration with no potential halt for Microsoft platforms to catch up. Apple is very keen on mobile use of its products in higher education, and is very much willing to send representatives to a campus to explore new ways of integrating mobile and AR technologies into curricula.[4]

Special Libraries

Special libraries are in the most unique position with AR: their user base is highly targeted and generally narrower in focus in terms of needs and desires. For the purposes of this section, it is important to focus specifically on special libraries that are their own separate entities rather than special libraries affiliated or housed within larger academic libraries, as these often tend to take on characteristics of the academic libraries themselves. Because of their size, these small special libraries often face limited resources as well as considerable budgetary restrictions. For many special libraries, the strategy behind AR purchases and development is very simple: make no investment until users request a particular piece of software or hardware. Letting users be the sole driving force behind AR development is a good strategy to protect against any fads that may arise in the AR universe sapping hard-earned fund-raising dollars. Approaching the board of directors of a small special library with numerous examples and case studies is the very best place to begin work in this vein.

If special library administrators are interested in experimenting, there are many freely available AR apps and development platforms that special libraries can consider launching to provide users with basic information via QR codes for particular building locations and collections. Hiring an intern to develop the content for the information is a good way to bridge the funding gap between needing to test the usefulness of AR tools and not having the financial support to restructure a specifically targeted staff position; this technology is still mostly underutilized. If an AR visualization project is seen as a promising addition to your collection (in the case of museum and archives libraries, for example), consult and visit with other institutions who can demonstrate their current implementations as a way to be successful right from the start.

EXAMPLES OF SUCCESSFUL IMPLEMENTATION

ShelvAR

Miami University of Ohio has developed an augmented reality app that can help librarians and other library professionals find misshelved books and return them to their proper homes. The app, called ShelvAR, is the collaborative brainchild of MU computer science professor Bo Brinkman. The ShelvAR app allows the user to view a shelf of books through the screen of a mobile device or tablet. Correctly shelved books are highlighted with a green check mark, while incorrectly shelved books are highlighted with a red *X*.[5] While the app is marketed primarily toward public libraries, its potential usefulness is practically universal across library types. The initial prototype requires books to be tagged with bar-code stickers (which correspond to call numbers) in order to be recognized and sorted by the app; this aspect of the software presents some financial restriction as well as time limitations. ShelvAR is unique, however, in its intended audience: it is one of the few successful AR endeavors that has deliberately been marketed toward library professionals rather than patrons.

Tagwhat

The Virginia Beach Public Library was selected as a pilot test partner for Tagwhat, a mobile storytelling app. The Tagwhat app, developed by a Colorado-based media company, uses augmented-reality technology so that users can access location-based stories. If a reader is in Virginia Beach and wants to go on a historical walking tour, they can use Tagwhat to view their surroundings through the screen of their mobile devices, and stories about their specific location will appear on the screen. Cynthia Hart, virtual librarian, and Nicole McGee, Emerging Technologies librarian at VBPL, created video, audio, and photo content for the app using their library's local history collection, as well as anecdotes from local residents. As VBPL director Marcy Sims perfectly sums up in an interview with the Virginia Library Association: "Our partnership with Tagwhat allows residents and visitors to access our local history collection in a unique, relevant way. . . . It also illustrates how libraries are pioneers in adopting emerging technologies."[6]

WolfWalk

The WolfWalk app is a virtual guide to the history of North Carolina State University designed for mobile devices. With the app, users can take a historical walking tour of the NC State campus using a location-aware campus map. Users can also browse over one thousand historical photographs provided by the NCSU Libraries Special Collections Research Center. The initial mobile web–based version of WolfWalk was launched in March 2010, and worked across a range of mobile devices, including iPhones, iPods, and Android-based smartphones.[7] Similar to the potential uses of location-aware AR apps within public libraries, apps such as WolfWalk provide a variety of unique learning opportunities in an academic setting. Whether the user in question is a new freshman on campus or a senior looking to immerse herself in campus history, these virtual walking tours allow students to experience their school's campus, as well as the historical collections, in interactive and creative ways.

The SCARLET Project

The Special Collections using Augmented Reality to Enhance Learning and Teaching (SCARLET) Project—sponsored by MIMAS (University of Manchester, UK)—aims to use augmented-reality technology to expose students to digitized primary-source materials such as original literary manuscripts and rare first editions. The SCARLET mobile app not only allows students to view digitized images of primary source materials, but also provides additional related content (text, images, audio) to go along with the digitized objects themselves.[8] With potential uses in both academic and special library collections, the SCARLET app provides a one-stop-shopping opportunity for students to view rare primary-source materials and helpful supplementary content, and at the same time still maintaining the physical integrity and stability of the physical collections themselves. These aspects provide rare opportunities for research and discovery not currently offered to the same extent by any other existing research tool. This type of app can be a welcome addition to any academic or special library that specializes in historical collections or rare materials.

MAKING AR MATTER IN RESEARCH AND DISCOVERY

The Needle in the Haystack

The way many potential researchers initially interact with AR is through the simple discovery of information useful in their day-to-day lives. A future researcher is taught and learns to become accustomed to the complexities of mixed-methods research-design techniques and linear regression software; of coding qualitative survey responses; and of manipulating online database interfaces. Yet AR interface skills are commonly acquired through the casual use of mobile phones and tablets; AR understanding and utilization is still too new to have moved much into curricular instruction. Say a future researcher is sitting with his phone or tablet and needs a hotel or a restaurant. He quickly checks his app store for something to augment the reality of his situation to help him find what he needs. The moment he downloads a popular mobile app such as Google Goggles, Layar, Augmented Car Finder, or Acrossair will do more to immediately teach this future researcher about AR than any instruction offered by many libraries or college courses today.

Urban areas provide much potential for using spontaneous mobile app AR because the most common search in urban areas is for specific vendors of merchandise and services among clusters of many, many options. Like books and other library resources stacked on shelves, urban areas are good foils for libraries where researchers need to find the proverbial needle in the haystack; that is, the one singular item within a cluster of potential useful outlets. AR helps users navigate through the problems of large clusters of information. This is where the bridge between the spontaneous need for everyday services and merchandise discovered through mobile apps can be ported to the research world. Research needs are generally much more purposeful and targeted in scope; apps are good for research because of the occasional serendipitous benefits that are commonly not acknowledged.

Behind the Curtain: Natural-Content AR

AR has the potential to reveal what constantly exists and is in front of a user at any given moment as the user is in motion and interacting with her environment. Simply put, users experience many circumstances and phenomena that are not perceived through the conscious mind. Acting as a sort of sixth sense, AR can reveal what is around a user beyond what the ordinary five senses detect moment by moment. Mobile apps such as iOnRoad, Spyglass, 3D Compass+, Augmented Colors, and Sun Seeker reveal "natural content" not created by humans, but useful to all in their search to understand the world around them. Details on each of these apps are listed in table 2.2 below.

AR tools such as these are a step along the path from leisure activity and casual learning to purpose-driven research work, as each of the aforementioned are best

TABLE 2.2
Augmented Reality Apps

App Name	Functionality
iOnRoad	By way of a dash-mounted smartphone, gauges distance between cars, travel speed, and travel direction
Spyglass	Includes an inclinometer, angular calculator, gyrocompass, sextant and other directional tools for hikers and other adventure enthusiasts.
3D Compass+	Combines features of popular mapping apps with a compass and a business locator
Augmented Colors	Gives RGB and hex values for colors captured through a mobile device camera lens
Sun Seeker	Shows the solar path of a given location, along with sunrise and -set times, a solar direction map, and the sun's elevation for any hour, day, or year
SloPro	Provides high-speed video recording and slow-motion playback at 1000fps for deeper analysis

applied toward strategic planning, business proposals, and problem solving in the pursuit of hypothesis testing. Each can be downloaded to mobile devices used for checkout in any library, giving users a new perspective to the outside world.

AR in Research Activities

In order to make AR useful for research activities, libraries can best strategize their future AR tool purchases and instruction schedules by analyzing ways in which their users seek to solve problems and answer research questions. If a researcher needs art and design information on color patterns, for example, libraries gain a creditable stake in the AR research game by introducing that researcher to apps that provide not only links and references to secondary research sources, but also to AR tools that can provide the capture and recording of color information. If a researcher's hypotheses center around how users will respond to a particular piece of round furniture versus a similar square piece of furniture in their homes or offices, recommendations from the library for rental furniture vendors may not be as appropriate as recommending the use of the Metaio platform (www.metaio .com), which simulates objects and/or people placed inside of a photograph of the location or space.

TABLE 2.3
Recommended Research AR Tablet Setup and Pricing (Apple Platform)

Hardware/Software	Price
iPad Mini 16GB	$258/10-pack
Statistics Pro	$0.99
Augment	Free
SloPro	Free
Augmented Colors	Free
Numbers	$9.99
Ripped from Reality	$1.99

By collecting primary-source data through AR tools, users have the potential to use simulated reality in a very rapid and inexpensive way not seen in the research realm since the introduction and mass adoption of mobile devices in the consumer marketplace. Considering that 56 percent of Americans now own at least one smartphone, libraries teaching and supporting the use of these devices is clearly advantageous.[9] With the price of basic devices such as the iPad Mini and Nexus 7 in the $200 range for bulk institutional purchases, academic and public libraries alike can realistically expect to purchase and circulate these devices for research users looking to capture data in easy and slick new ways. Cheap mobile tablets all provide basic recording features for qualitative researchers conducting interviews, or those looking to capture instances and evidence of change in an environment or test subject over time. By spending just under $20 in key applications for a seven-inch basic mobile tablet, a library researcher can get up and rolling toward practically and pragmatically using AR technologies without worry of confusion. (See table 2.3.)

Pressure to provide AR and mobile technologies in libraries is mounting as sales of these devices in the commercial marketplace soar. Libraries looking to not invest too much money in AR technologies—which can commonly be seen as an entertainment fads—can consider the aforementioned recommendation as a pilot response project that will prove that the library is not behind the times in embracing the new mobile reality. Piloting the use of AR for research purposes can yield useful data to indicate and guide your library's appropriate levels of investment going forward.

MAKING THE NUMBERS WORK:
WHERE TO INVEST AND WHY

With all that is currently being discussed and planned for AR technologies in the consumer realm, the most important question for libraries is, where to invest? Libraries that want to play a larger role in their community—and in their patrons' consciousness—need to make strategic investments in AR technologies, not just throw money at devices and software in the hopes that patrons will flock to use them. There are AR technologies that users may need, and then there are those that they want. Achieving a balance between patron desire and budgetary constraint becomes most appropriate in light of austerity and accountability calls from public granting bodies and tax/tuition payers after the great recession of 2008. If libraries do not invest in AR, they will be considered out of date, and those who already think libraries are outmoded will have another reason to exclaim their disdain. This leaves libraries with few options but to dip in and play with what is coming next in AR, to show once again that they have a seat at the table in a world where Internet-based technologies challenge their very existence.

Investing in Yourself: Pilot Programs and Research

For many libraries, the best initial investment is to buy a piece of AR equipment and/or software and give it to a set of core users to gauge their reaction for future investment and rollout. Identifying this core-user test base, however, can be tricky. Libraries with only one or two tech-savvy individuals on staff may find that these two people are not the best choice for identifying how the typical patron will react to AR technologies. Then again, the staff members who do not possess a high level of intuition for technology could take too long to train to be good participants in a pilot project. Each library director should, therefore, be very close to the decision-making process for an AR pilot project. In some cases, working with boards or higher-level stakeholders to pick the best pilot candidates is the best way to provide a solid rationale for experimenting in the first place. AR may or may not be a standard service of libraries in the future; caution is necessary when reflecting on how to spend budgetary dollars. If support flows from the top of an organization downward for investment in AR, there will be fewer questions later on the process regarding how AR fits within the library's mission.

For small/medium libraries, a proposed pilot project can be found in table 2.4. For larger libraries, an AR pilot project focusing on a wider audience will be more appropriate; see table 2.5.

TABLE 2.4

AR Pilot Project for Small and Medium Libraries: Archives Alive

Pilot Project Title	Archives Alive
AR Test Software/Hardware	String
Software/Hardware Functionality	Embeds 3-D imagery inside of real-world pictures and objects as a way to provide rich content without creating 3-D diagrams and displays
Software Cost	Free
Hardware Cost	$399 for a tablet device
Personnel Cost	Minimal
Brief Project Description	Working with student artists, library and archives staff create 3-D images of artifacts contained in archival collections that users may want to touch but that are too brittle for frequent handling. String will allow users to simulate the experience of fully interacting with archival materials while supporting preservation.
Pilot Project Team	1 administrative staff lead 1 digital design student 2 patrons

TABLE 2.5

AR Pilot Project for Large Libraries: VAR Gamer Space

Pilot Project Title	VAR (Virtual and Augmented Reality) Gamer Space
AR Test Software/Hardware	Oculus Rift and Halo 2
Software/Hardware Functionality	Complete next-generation virtual/augmented reality gaming headset attached to a high-end PC gaming console and projection display
Software Cost	$10
Hardware Cost	$300 for Rift $2,000 for a PC $2,000 for projection and sound equipment
Personnel Cost	Existing systems staff will be required to work multiple hours for software modifications.
Brief Project Description	Half-Life 2 is a very popular first-person shooter (FPS) game for PC and other platforms. Now with Oculus Rift mod support, this game can be an ideal draw for patrons to try AR in a dedicated space within their libraries. Patron traffic flow may need to be aggressively managed if the VAR Gamer Space becomes popular.
Pilot Project Team	1–2 administrative staff leads 1+ systems staff 2 test patrons

Spending under $500 in small and medium-sized libraries, and just under $5,000 in larger libraries with larger budgets, can bring each institution type into the business of testing, piloting and eventually delivering AR technologies to their patrons. Bottom line: this technology is very new and in very early development for the consumer market. Any library of any size and type that willingly takes on a pilot program in AR will be a pioneer the moment their particular project is launched.

Many libraries are talking about what AR can do, with most of the focus being targeted in mobile apps that can simply be recommended for users. A much more aggressive and progressive approach is the lending of software and hardware that, in some cases, is partially made by library staff themselves. A library with the mission to be on the cutting edge of the information landscape is a natural fit for investment in AR. Without at least one AR offering, any library that claims to be high-tech will question its strategic planning until investment in this technology is made.

Taking Risks for Technological Relevancy

Libraries looking to invest in AR are, therefore, looking to place themselves as models for others to follow in the future. With the Oculus Rift, Oakley Airwave, Google Glass, and Samsung OLED televisions allowing two viewers to watch different content on the same screen, and countless apps for Droid, Windows, and Apple devices in the pipeline, AR is coming to everyone faster and faster each day. Libraries must take chances with these technologies, along with the rest of the world, until there are clear valuable choices among the many failures.

PREDICTIONS, RECOMMENDATIONS, AND CONCLUSION

There are indications within the library community suggesting that AR technology will prove to be a force to be reckoned with in the coming years. The 2011 Horizon Report cites augmented reality as one of several "technologies to watch." [10] The 2011 Report estimates a two- to three-year window before AR enters the mainstream. Ironically, AR entered into the conversation once more in the 2013 Horizon Report, this time in the form of "wearable" technologies, akin to the Google Glass project. [11] Whether wearable or on a mobile handset, augmented reality has been and will likely continue to be an exciting topic of conversation, both within libraries and beyond. If predictions regarding the popularity of AR in the public market prove accurate, it seems reasonable to expect that numerous library implementations will ultimately follow as consumers lead the charge through the nonstop downloading of apps and hardware.

In the end, each library's ability to implement augmented reality into their range of services will depend on a variety of factors, chief among them budgetary restrictions. Larger institutions with substantial budgets and more financial flexibility will continue to be among the first to implement AR technologies. The overwhelming financial limitations that smaller institutions face are coupled with a sense of anxiety over the possibility of "failure to launch," or failure of implementation. Impulsive or imprudent investment decisions on technologies still in their infancy are certainly to be discouraged; any library must weigh these practical factors when choosing whether or not to invest in a particular technology. In some ways, however, this fear of failure has placed a stranglehold over libraries' ability to be innovative and creative. Over the last several years the library community has made great strides in combating this mentality, particularly with the makerspace movement. Libraries of all shapes and sizes are embracing their roots as places where users can go to experience new and different ways to learn and discover, but without the need to tie this discovery directly to reading in all cases. If libraries can continue to balance innovation and creativity with fiscal responsibility—and to balance the myriad ways their patrons discover and learn— AR technologies will definitely play a critical role in the progress of information discovery and the value of libraries within their communities.

NOTES

1. Tracey Wilen-Daugenti, "Higher Education Trends & Statistics, Issue 1," Cisco, accessed October 1, 2013, www.cisco.com/web/about/ac79/edu/trends/issue01 .html.

2. Becky Hayes, "You've Been Warned." *USA Today College*, May 15, 2012, www .usatodayeducate.com/staging/index.php/pulse/youve-been-warned. Accessed October 1, 2013; Amy Harwath. "Emergency Text Alert System Inconsistent Across College Campuses." CU-CitizenAccess, April 25, 2013, www.cu-citizenaccess.org/ content/emergency-text-alert-system-inconsistent-across-college-campuses.

3. Judy Bloxham, "Augmented Reality in Education: Teaching Tool or Passing Trend?" *Higher Education Network* (blog), *The Guardian,* February 11, 2013, www.theguardian .com/higher-education-network/blog/2013/feb/11/augmented-reality-teaching-tool -trend.

4. "Apple—Education—Become an Apple Campus Rep at Your College," Apple, accessed October 12, 2013, www.apple.com/education/campusreps/; E. Booker, "Apple's Education Phenomenon: iPad," *InformationWeek*, December 28, 2012,

www.informationweek.com/education/mobility/apples-education-phenomenon -ipad/240145351.

5. "Miami University Augmented Reality Research Group (MU ARGG!)," Miami University of Ohio, accessed October 10, 2013, www.users.muohio.edu/ brinkmwj/ar.

6. "Library Tapped as Pilot Partner for Augmented Reality Mobile App Tagwhat," Virginia Library·Association, July 14, 2011, www.vla.org/2011/07/14/library -tapped-as-pilot-partner-for-augmented-reality-mobile-app-tagwhat.

7. "WolfWalk." North Carolina State University Libraries, accessed October 10, 2013, www.lib.ncsu.edu/dli/projects/wolfwalk.

8. "Special Collections in the Age of the App." MIMAS, University of Manchester, August 25, 2011, http://mimas.ac.uk/news/2011/08/scarlet.

9. Aaron Smith, "56% of American Adults Are Now Smartphone Owners," PewResearch Internet Project, June 5, 2013, pewinternet.org/Reports/2013/Smartphone-Owner ship-2013/Findings.aspx.

10. L. Johnson et al., *The 2011 Horizon Report* (Austin, Texas: The New Media Consortium, 2011), https://net.educause.edu/ir/library/pdf/HR2011.pdf.

11. L. Johnson et al., *The 2013 Horizon Report* (Austin: The New Media Consortium, 2013), https://net.educause.edu/ir/library/pdf/HR2013.pdf.

Libraries and Archives Augmenting the World

William Denton

The future is already here—it's just not very evenly distributed.
—William Gibson

"LUNCH WITH ZOIA"

Zoia was finishing her morning shift at the ref desk when the young man came up and said he couldn't find a book on the shelf. He wasn't wearing.

"Do you have the call number?" she asked. He held up his phone and showed the book in the catalogue: it was in the QCs, which were always hard to find. Her glasses recognized the small code on the page and popped up a small window to her left. The status showed it was on the shelf—at least, it wasn't checked out, hadn't been in seven months, and had been shelf-read three days ago when a wearing student assistant passed by.

"It should be there," she said. "Come on, I'll help you find it." If the student was wearing she'd have helped him install the library's app, because then he could have hit "Take me there" and it would have drawn arrows along the floor, up the stairs, and behind the offices, and then highlighted the section of the shelf where the book sat. Zoia herself didn't need that, of course, so she dismissed the window. They chatted as they went looking. He was in science studies. She could see from her calendar that there was a talk from a visiting prof in that area on Friday; he hadn't heard of it and was glad to know.

Back downstairs, two messages showed quietly: the second printer was out of paper, and George would be ten minutes late for lunch because the subways were still down from the storm two days earlier. She dismissed the printer warning—the students would see it—and sent a quick "no problem" to George. On the way out of the library, she saw the two student assistants, both wearing employee glasses: one was heading for the printer, and the other was charging out books by looking at student cards and the spines of the books.

Zoia was meeting George at a pub a ten-minute walk from her university that was also easy to get to from George's public library, especially when the subways were working. She enjoyed the view as she left the university: she ran Adblock Lens, which she'd customized so it disabled every possible ad on campus as well as in the bus stops and on the billboards on the city streets. Sometimes she replaced them with live content, but today she just had the blanked spaces colored softly to blend in with what was around them. No ads, just a lot of beige and brown, slightly glitchy.

On top of that view she ran Architectivist, a new app that Ebscovier was beta testing. It overlaid information on buildings: identifying the address, it could search in city and other databases to find physical facts, ownership records, and tax values; image recognition was good at determining the architectural style; sometimes it would give biographies of the architect; and for well-known buildings, it could overlay the whole thing with 3-D photo–based recreations of how it looked over time. The Odeon was Zoia's favorite—the marquee showed that Sinatra had performed in the early forties and Funkadelic in 1976. The app was good, but it cost too much and would be impossible to integrate with the university's single sign-on system. She'd recommend against buying it. Anyway, only about 10 percent of the students wore. They could use the mobile version like everyone else for now. The whole thing grated on her nerves: almost all the data was from public sources, and they had to spend heavy annual fees to have it sold back to them.

Zoia cut down a shaded side street. She ran a new app built by students in a finance and environmental studies course: it showed a large 3-D model of the nearest best cheapest fast food. Two blocks ahead floated a large falafel. She looked behind her—there was a gyro a block back. This was a good app. It would get picked up by lots of people all over town, students and not, especially clubbers. She plussed the falafel because she knew the restaurant and liked it.

At the pub, the menu was enhanced, so they ordered through her glasses, and the waiter came by with their drinks a couple of minutes later and said the food would be ready soon. George shared a new app the public library had bought to go with the materials it had for ambulance driver certification. Zoia's phone ran it once she decrypted access to her account, and they tried it while they waited. George couldn't afford glasses on a city salary, so he ran it on his phone. He threw a small marker on the table, a city popped up, and they each drove a little ambulance around, getting to emergencies quickly without many mistakes, but then they got bored and started running into cars and the app shut itself down and scolded them.

"Good thing we already have jobs," George said.

An hour later they had to get back to work. "I've got a thing, let me check . . ." Zoia said. She brought up her calendar to see if the consultation at 2:30 had supplied any details yet. The hour had turned red! "Uh-oh, it's that grad student I was telling you about. It'll be a long one. Well, see you Saturday."

She shut down everything except Adblock on the way back, walking slowly and enjoying the fall afternoon. When she entered the campus again, she brought up the work apps. Messages started fading in on the left, and to the right she could see the printer had jammed and the ref desk was unexpectedly busy and Robin needed backup. Back to work. At least she knew where to get a good gyro.

29

GETTING STARTED

Before we begin, if you haven't read *Rainbows End* by Vernor Vinge (Tor, 2006), then get your hands on a copy right now. It's mandatory reading for anyone interesting in augmented reality—especially in our field, because it describes the wildest book-digitization project ever. It's science fiction. These days we *live* in science fiction.

Now take out your smartphone and install and run Layar.[1] Tap the screen to make it scan this page. You'll see buttons and images floating a little above it. You can hear me say hello, see a picture of Saturn, read what @ala_lita has been tweeting recently, and more. I crammed a lot into a small space, but think what you could do like this with a handout, a poster, or even a wall in your library.

Next, install and run Junaio. Hold up your phone and look around. You'll probably see something like figure 3.1, with little icons floating in space. Your phone knows where you're standing and which direction you're pointing it, and Junaio uses that to find points of interest around you that are listed in Wikipedia with latitude and longitude. Press one to find out about it.

These are examples of augmented reality (AR): virtual objects added by computer to the real world around us.

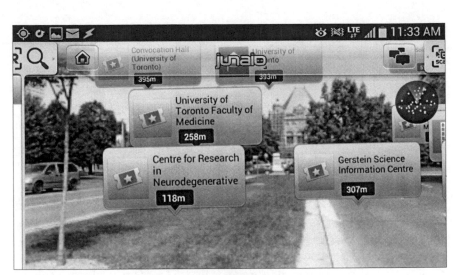

FIGURE 3.1
Junaio View. North Along University Avenue
at College Street in Downtown Toronto

But actually that's not true: these aren't *really* augmented reality, the way AR will be. As first steps in AR, these apps and the others I'll cover are powerful. Compared to the AR we'll have by 2017, they're boring. It's difficult to talk about AR right now because things are changing very quickly. This is especially true with AR glasses. Some of the technology in this chapter will be out of date when you read it, but the general directions will, I hope, be relevant for a while.[2]

WHAT IS AUGMENTED REALITY?

Ronald Azuma's 1997 definition of AR is the simplest and clearest to me: "AR allows the user to see the real world, with virtual objects superimposed upon or composited with the real world. Therefore, AR supplements reality, rather than completely replacing it" (which virtual reality does). He set out three characteristics that a system must have to be augmented reality: "1) Combines real and virtual; 2) Interactive in real time; 3) Registered in 3-D" (that last meaning accurately placed in a 3D coordinate system: poor registration means virtual objects wiggle or jump around).[3]

There are other ways of thinking about AR. Milgram and Kishino set out "mixed reality" as a continuum spanning the completely real to the entirely virtual, with augmented reality closer to one end and augmented virtuality (virtual environments including real objects) toward the other.[4] Steve Mann, who has been wearing computer-enhanced eyewear for decades, is working on "augmediated reality," which will let us "deliberately diminish, augment, and more generally re-map and modify reality perception":[5] we could subtract things from the real world that we don't want to see (such as advertisements), or change things so we can see them better (such as adjusting the camera's dynamic range so that something as bright as welding is as easy to see in clear detail). And Vinge is what really brings it all to life.[6]

A NOTE ABOUT PRIVACY

Using augmented reality involves sharing your location and using your camera to see what is around you. I won't go into the privacy aspects, but keep it in mind as you read. If you wore AR glasses, how would you feel about your position and camera feed possibly being known to others? What do you think about being recorded as a background figure by the cameras other people are wearing? If your library has a policy about photography in the building now, how will you handle someone wearing AR glasses? Steve Mann's idea of "sousveillance"[7] is a good place to enter the debate on this issue, and Wikipedia has many links about it.

FOUR METHODS OF AUGMENTING REALITY

There are different ways of classifying types of AR, but for our purposes let's say there are four: geolocation and markers are the main ways right now, but glasses and the physical environment are coming along very quickly. I'll discuss each, with examples of and pointers on how to start to make your own AR.

Geolocation

Geolocated AR is what you saw in Junaio (junaio.com). Smartphones know where you are, which direction you're facing, and the angle you're holding your phone. With that, an app can determine what should be added to the camera view to augment what is around you. There are problems, though: GPS isn't exact, the registration is not fine enough, you may be identified only to within meters of where you are, things may jump around, and GPS doesn't work inside buildings.

To see a geolocated view in Layar (layar.com), go into "Geo Layers" and search for "Tweeps Around" (for Twitter) or "Instagram" to see who has been posting to

31

these sites near you (and has been sharing their exact location). It's very interesting to be in a busy area when something is going on and to see how people all around you have been posting to social sites. Wikitude (wikitude.com) begins with a menu of different kinds of channels you can view, including nearby activity, Wikipedia entries, restaurants, transit, and more. As with Layar and Junaio, you can search or browse categories, but Wikitude does the best job of presenting the options attractively.

Worth noting is Mixare (mixare.org) because it is a free and open-source AR app (licensed under the GPL). By default it displays nearby points of interest from Wikipedia, Twitter, and OpenStreetMap, and other sources can be added. It does not seem to be under active development, but I hope that changes, because we very much need good open AR applications.

To make your own geolocated channels on these apps is free but takes some programming skills. You'll configure it on the vendor's website, then set up a web service under your control that takes in information such as latitude and longitude and returns points of interest (POIs) in the format the vendor wants (there is no standardization on this yet). They all have documentation on their websites and usually include many examples. The programming is not difficult, and if you have some geolocated data to experiment with, then I encourage you to try to get something working.[8] (There is a third-party application called BuildAR (buildar .com) that gives you an easy interface to build and manage POIs for Junaio, for a monthly fee.)

A special note about Historypin (historypin.com), which is barely augmented reality but is a site all archives should know about.[9] Users can upload photographs, video, audio, and text to the site and pin the media to a location and a time. It's most fun to work with photographs taken on streets, because Historypin has a tool that lets you use Google Street View to layer an old photograph on top of what the street looks like now. You can view these in a browser or on location with their app. My York University colleague Anna St.Onge pinned some historical photos of Toronto's Kensington Market, such as one of the Bellevue Nut Shop and Soda Bar in 1955.[10] I went down there and overlaid the old photo on top of the camera view, and figure 3.2 is what I saw.

Historypin meets only one of Azuma's three criteria. And yet . . . it's a step along the path. Some day in the future you'll be able to walk down the street and see the past as it was, all around on all sides. But it will take a lot of work to get there: digitization, image analysis, registering the photos accurately stitching together multiple photos to make a 3-D view, and more.

FIGURE 3.2
1955 overlaid on top of 2013. It was difficult to line things up exactly
because I was standing in the middle of a busy street.

Markers

Fiducial markers (the word derives from the Latin for "trust" or "confidence") are objects predefined and ready for an AR application to recognize and use as a point of reference. Sometimes special markers are made that look like a cross between a QR code and a Jackson Pollock painting: they are visually rich, and not only can an application recognize them in any setting, it can also calculate the angle at which they are viewed. But any object can be turned into a marker: a page in a book (as with this chapter), a poster, a sign, or a product package. The application adds an augmentation on top of the marker and can allow you to see it from all sides, by moving the marker or yourself.

Layar, Junaio, and Wikitude all work with markers, often used for advertising. Look on their websites for examples (you can just scan a marker off your monitor to try it; you don't need to print it out). There are a number of other basic apps available, the best being Augment (http://augmentedev.com/), which uses markers to show 3-D objects that can be moved, rotated, and resized. Something different is Word Lens (http://questvisual.com/us/), which translates words in real time as they appear in the camera view. Such functionality will probably become a part of all AR systems. An educational example is Daqri's Anatomy 4D (www.daqri.com/project/anatomy-4d/), which uses a marker to anchor a 3-D human body and let

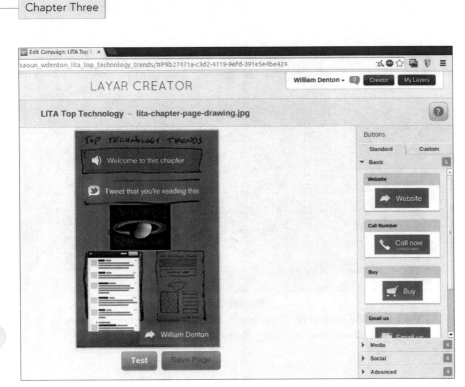

FIGURE 3.3
Layar Creator's drag-and-drop interface is easy to use.

the user look at bones, nerves, the circulatory or digestive systems, and more, from all angles.

Using markers to augment print is by far the easiest way to make your own AR. It's worth trying, and it takes only about half an hour to get something working. The three apps mention all have their own creation tools: Layar Creator (layar .com/creator/; see fig. 3.3) and Wikitude Studio (studio.wikitude.com) both work in the browser, and Junaio has desktop and smartphone applications. There are some differences between the systems, but generally they all allow you to augment an image with text, images, 3-D models, hyperlinks, video, audio, and live HTML. Pricing varies, and Layar lets you publish ad-supported pages for free.

Developing your own native application that uses image recognition for a custom 3-D AR experience requires a software development kit (SDK). The leading AR SDK is Qualcomm's Vuforia (https://www.vuforia.com), which integrates with the Unity 3D game engine (www.unity3d.com). Vuforia comes at no charge but is not free software and has a restrictive license. With it, you would be able to build an app that recognized markers and objects and added any augment you wanted on top of them. You could also do this with OpenCV (www.opencv.org), the best free computer vision system, but it would take more work. Layar, Junaio, and Wikitude also have software development kits (SDKs) available for a fee or with restrictions.

Glasses

AR glasses seem to finally be ready to come onto the market for regular consumers. They combine very small cameras and displays: the mounted cameras recognize objects and hand gestures; a computer accurately locates these in space and calculates the augmentations to be added; then special displays in the glasses show the augments where the wearer's eyes see them and put everything all together into one. Glasses such as this can offer true augmented reality.

There are three systems worth following right now—though who knows how they will fare, and others will certainly come along. The first, Google Glass (www .google.com/glass/), isn't AR. When wearing Glass, you see a rectangle of content up and to the right in your field of vision: you can see a map, send a text, talk to someone through a video feed, and more. It's a remarkable piece of technology, but it's a hands-free phone, not AR. Yet.

The next two promise real AR. Unfortunately, neither is available as I write, but both should be out when this book is published. Vuzix (www.vuzix.com) has been working in the field for a while, but the M100 Smart Glasses are their first AR product aimed at regular folks. Meta, a startup with Steve Mann as its chief scientist, is making META.01 (www.spaceglasses.com; available September 2014). There are demo videos on both sites, and probably more will be there when you read this, so have a look for the most current information. If what Meta shows in their video actually works—two people playing chess on a virtual chessboard, for example, and someone designing an object in the air with an AR design program, then literally passing it over to a 3-D printer to become real—then it will be a huge step forward.

To develop apps for glasses, check the vendor websites for SDKs. Advanced programming skills are required. Eventually, I hope, there will be user-friendly tools that will let us manage AR environments in these systems—the equivalent of how easy WordPress and a few plugins make it to manage a website now.

Glasses will attract the most attention for AR and offer the most promise for what it can do. What glasses will be like in 2017 is impossible to predict, but until networked contact lenses are available that can show information right on your eye (which researchers are working on), glasses are where the most interesting and life-changing AR will happen.

The Physical Environment

A fourth way of doing AR is in the physical environment. Motion sensors can detect your movements in space and allow you to control virtual objects on a computer screen with gestures. If they show a camera view of you and what's around you, you can see yourself mixing the real and virtual on screen—perhaps grabbing and moving an object that seems to be floating in front of you. Motion detection can be combined with projectors showing things on surfaces around you; for example, displaying a keyboard you can type on and then dismiss.

Two new examples of such motion-detection systems are the Leap Motion (www .leapmotion.com), a small USB-connected device that can detect the positions of your hands and fingers with submillimeter accuracy; and Thalmic's Myo (www .thalmic.com/myo/), due in 2014, an armband that reads your muscle movements for computer control with gestures. Glasses also do gesture recognition, of course, but these devices may offer much better accuracy. And perhaps they will be combined: you could wear a Myo on your forearm to help control what you see through your glasses.

It's possible to use simple markers to do AR on screen with the physical environment right now. The ARToolKit (www.sourceforge.net/projects/artoolkit/) is a GPL system for doing this, and there are many variations online. Colleagues at York University built the SnapDragonAR system (www.futurestories.ca/ snapdragon/) to make it easy to do AR this way. It was used to interesting effect by Geoffrey Alan Rhodes in his talk "AR on AR: Occupying Virtual Space."[11]

CLOSED!

Practically everything I've mentioned so far is closed: closed-source and proprietary platforms. APIs (application programming interfaces) may be available but lock you in to one vendor's system. This makes it harder for libraries and archives to do AR. Today it means we need to do unnecessary work on duplicate platforms: presenting the same POIs on Layar and on Junaio means double work, for example. Picture what it will be like when we want to present an AR experience on two different kinds of glasses. Cross-platform development tools may be available, but they may cost a lot of money.

Library software vendors are notorious for charging for closed platforms today. Imagine if this gets worse. We need to use existing open standards and tools, support the development of necessary new ones, and make our content and source code available under open licenses. If we can't write our own applications, then by making our content easily available we will encourage people to use it in their own—the same as happens now on the open Web.

AR IN USE

Other chapters about AR in this book discuss what's going inside libraries.[12] Here are three directions going out.

The Bavarian State Library (Bayerische Staatsbibliothek, or BSB) made an iOS app about Ludwig II of Bavaria, "Ludwig II—Walking the Footsteps of the Fairytale King,"[13] that brings to life places and buildings in Munich and elsewhere that the mad king knew. It presents POIs near the user with supplementary information in text and multimedia, shows a 360-degree simulation of a building that no longer exists, and more. It's a wonderful example of a library pushing its material outside its walls and into the world where people can use it in place. (Inside the library they've done another interesting AR project, the 3D BSB Browser,[14] which uses gesture control and eye tracking to give the user an interactive 3-D digitized historical book—without requiring any glasses. See Ceynowa[15] for more about both.)

Special Collections Using Augmented Reality to Enhance Learning and Teaching, or SCARLET (teamscarlet.wordpress.com), is a project of several UK universities that is interesting for what it has done and also how it has been organized. The website explains,

> SCARLET addresses one of the principal obstacles to the use of Special Collections in teaching and learning—the fact that students must consult rare books, manuscripts and archives within the controlled conditions of library study rooms. The material is isolated from the secondary, supporting materials and the growing mass of related digital assets. This is an alien experience for students familiar with an information-rich, connected wireless world, and is a barrier to their use of Special Collections.[16]

In one project they used Junaio to make a channel to open up part of a large collection of social research. The website documents their work in detail.

To consider what archives might do with AR, it's worthwhile to look at what museums have done, since they generally have more money and more visitors.[17]

The Museum of London's "Street Museum" app[18] highlights historical photos from their collection similar to Historypin. The Asian Art Museum in San Francisco had an iOS app[19] made for its *China's Terracotta Warriors* exhibit in early 2013; the main feature is that you can see an "animated life-sized 3D terracotta warrior." Most notably the British Museum has done several Junaio-based AR projects aimed at children, and Shelley Mannion's 2012 talk "Beyond Cool: Making Mobile Augmented Reality Work for Museum Education" gives a good overview of them, including lessons learned. The augmented camera view was especially exciting for users, she says: "The biggest surprise with the AR activity was students' utter fascination with the live camera view. It was so entrancing that, from the moment the AR module went live halfway through the project, camera usage [for taking photos] on the phones dropped dramatically."[20]

TEN IMPLICATIONS FOR THE FUTURE

It's a mug's game to predict how augmented reality will go over the next three or four years, but here are some things we can do that will serve us well no matter how things end. I think AR will grow enormously, and if it does, these approaches will help. If it doesn't, we will have learned something, and we'll still be ready for whatever comes next.

1. Augmented reality glasses are where things will happen. When you can, get your hands on a pair and try them. It will be a worthwhile investment.
2. We must provide content in standard ways. APIs should be open and clearly documented. If content is available for use in platform A, it should be easily reused for platform B. Assume that whatever we're making will be out of date in a year or two and that we'll need to rewrite it or move it to a new platform. Building with standards and open code will make this easier; providing content for reuse by others under open licenses will too.
3. Archives and special collections are probably the best units to start trying out AR because they have unique content that can be brought to life in new ways, so have these staff do the pilot projects. These colleagues will have useful examples to show others who can apply

AR elsewhere. This experimentation might take place with basic things such as signs and handouts first, but how will AR be used in information literacy and in the research process? The IL librarians need to be thinking about this.

4. We need to put pressure on vendors to keep our needs in mind. They will eventually start to make AR apps—probably first in STEM and medicine—but such apps will be even less usable and harder to integrate into our systems than their mobile applications are now. And they will cost a lot. Ownership and licensing will be confused.

5. The technical skills required to do advanced AR are high, but basic AR today is very approachable and a good learning experience. Anyone interested should experiment with it. Building IT skills in libraries is a hard problem, and it's not going to get any easier. Be prepared to spend more time and money. This problem is not going to get any simpler.

6. We will grow with partners: community groups with their own special content; students and professors learning and teaching in new ways; local makerspaces with skills and tools. We have special knowledge, collections, and expertise that others will be interested in, and libraries are friendly, safe places to work together. We should get involved wherever AR is being worked on in our communities. Go to meetups. We can't make it all ourselves, and there are smart people out there.

7. Accessibility programs and policies will need to adapt.

8. Privacy and legal implications will be ever more important.

9. The divide will grow between those with the right hardware who can run the latest apps and those without who can't. We still need to provide full access to all resources to everyone. Some of your users will have the latest fancy glasses; others won't have Internet access at home. Academic librarians: can you lend out AR glasses on reserve when an instructor assigns an AR app for a class?

10. Though AR may not make huge changes quickly to what happens inside libraries or how people read or do research, we need to fit in with how the rest of world is going. Smartphones and social media may be a useful parallel: the core purposes of libraries are still the same as before Facebook and Twitter, but we are adapting to fit into a much-changed information landscape. We will need to do the same with AR, whatever that turns out to be.

39

MORE INFORMATION

Everything about AR is changing quickly, and this chapter will be out of date when you read it. To help fight this, I will maintain a web page at www.miskatonic .org/ar/lita that has links to everything mentioned in this chapter and to other AR resources of interest to librarians and archivists, including blogs and Twitter accounts. Right now Twitter is the best way to keep up with what's happening (my list of AR-related accounts at twitter.com/wdenton/ar is a good place to start.)

AR conferences are good sources to see who is talking about what, whether it's researchers or vendors, theory or applications. The major academic conference is the IEEE International Symposium on Mixed and Augmented Reality (ISMAR, www.ismar.net), but others, such as the IEEE Society on the Social Implications of Technology's (www.ieeessit.org) ISTAS (International Symposium on Technology and Society), are important. Practitioners go to the academic conferences, but more specifically there is the Augmented World Expo (augmentedworldexpo .com), which calls itself "the world's largest augmented reality trade show"; the Augmented Reality Summit (augmentedrealitysummit.com); and Metaio's insideAR (www.metaio.com/insidear/home/).

Standards are important. Libraries and archives have lots of our own standards that need to be integrated with the AR world, and AR needs its own standards, such as ARML from the Open Geospatial Consortium (opengeospatial.org). The grassroots AR Standards group (www.perey.com/ARStandards/) is working on this. For more about this and other discussion, see also the W3C Augmented Reality Community Group (www.w3.org/community/ar/).

NOTES

1. You may not have a smartphone, or it may not be able to run Layar or Junaio. If this happens to you reading this book, imagine the problems ahead for our users.

2. To keep up to date with current information, see my supporting web page at www .miskatonic.org/ar/lita. In print, see Gregory Kipper and Joseph Rampolla, *Augmented Reality: An Emerging Technologies Guide to AR*, Waltham, MA: Syngress, 2012. Kipper and Rampolla's work is a thorough overview of where AR was at, but it's already out of date as I write a few months after it was published.

3. Ronald T. Azuma, "A Survey of Augmented Reality," *Presence: Teleoperators and Virtual Environments* 6, no. 4 (August 1997): 2, www.ronaldazuma.com/papers/ARpresence .pdf.

4. Paul Milgram and Fumio Kishino, "A Taxonomy of Mixed Reality Visual Displays." *IEICE Transactions on Information Systems* E77-D, no. 12 (December 1994), http:// etclab.mie.utoronto.ca/people/paul_dir/IEICE94/ieice.html.

5. Steve Mann, "Augmediated Reality and 'McVeillance,'" *Steve Mann's Blog*. September 13, 2012, http://eyetap.blogspot.ca/2012/09/augmediated-reality-and-mcveillance .html. See also Steve Mann, "My 'Augmediated' Life: What I've Learned from 35 Years of Wearing Computerized Eyewear." *IEEE Spectrum*, March 1, 2013, http://spectrum .ieee.org/geek-life/profiles/steve-mann-my-augmediated-life.

6. Vernor Vinge, *Rainbows End* (New York: Tor, 2006).

7. Steve Mann, "Veillance and Reciprocal Transparency: Surveillance versus Sousveillance, AR Glass, Lifelogging, and Wearable Computing," paper presented at IEEE International Symposium on Technology and Society (ISTAS) 2013 conference, June 2013, http://wearcam.org/veillance/veillance.pdf.

8. I myself wrote Avoirdupois (github.com/wdenton/avoirdupois), a simple Ruby web service that drives Layar POIs, and Laertes (github.com/wdenton/avoirdupois), which brings together nearby tweets and points of interest from a Google Map.

9. There is a page for libraries, archives and museums at historypin.com/community/lams/.

10. See www.historypin.com/channels/view/id/5604123/#|map/index/#!/geo:43 .657111,-79.404512/zoom:20/dialog:16591017/tab:details.

11. See https://www.youtube.com/watch?v=SyAkUJCgDUk.

12. See also Jim Hahn, 2012, "Mobile Augmented Reality Applications for Library Services," *New Library World* 113 (9/10): 429–438, doi:10.1108/03074801211273902.

13. See www.bayerische-landesbibliothek-online.de/ludwigii-appeng.

14. See Bayeriche Staatsbibilothek's October 2012 YouTube video, "Der 3D-BSB-Explorer —Handschriften lesen in 3D," https://www.youtube.com/watch?v=eyPRjMerCkU.

15. Klaus Ceynowa, "Augmented Reality, Location Based Services and More: Innovative User Scenarios for Library Content," February 2013, https://www.youtube.com/ watch?v=gp9tAzTLUXU.

16. "About the Project," SCARLET (Special Collections Using Augmented Reality to Enhance Learning and Teaching), accessed August 15, 2012, http://teamscarlet .wordpress.com/about.

17. You can see a lot with a YouTube or Vimeo search for *"augmented reality museum"*— video always helps make the experience more understandable.

18. See www.museumoflondon.org.uk/Resources/app/you-are-here-app/home.html.

19. See www.magma-studios.com/ar/aam.

20. Shelley Mannion, "Beyond Cool: Making Mobile Augmented Reality Work for Museum Education," April 2012, www.museumsandtheweb.com/mw2012/papers/ beyond_cool_making_mobile_augmented_reality_wo.

The Future of Cloud-Based Library Systems

Steven K. Bowers and Elliot J. Polak

The current and future trends of library services and the software for delivering those services are intertwined. It may be debatable which comes first, but the two are inseparable and necessarily affect each other. It is definite, however, that the limits of the now-aging integrated library system (ILS) software model are constraining the presence of the library within the new reality of the Internet and interconnected World Wide Web.

Utilities for library system cooperation, such as OCLC, have served as a mechanism for facilitating resource sharing, built around a core of shared record keeping for tracking holdings within member libraries. Whether they are called cloud-based ILS or library services platforms, developing and future systems will move beyond shared library resources on shelves to establishing a shared technological infrastructure for supporting all that libraries do.

Library platform systems are under development or in early adoption, and while it is not necessary to name specific companies and their product offerings, it is certainly worth examining common platform features and designs that are planned or have already been implemented. Cloud-based systems have a hosted technological infrastructure, which also allows for staff and public access via a web browser. A platform solution will provide means for management of all library systems, including circulation, cataloging, acquisitions, serials, electronic resources, authentication, the public interface, and analytics for data in the system.

New platform systems currently in use, as well as those under development, are intended to be built on a somewhat common suite of services. As with older

ILS, these platforms already manage bibliographic and holdings data for library materials, supporting cataloging and circulation functions. In various stages of development are associated acquisitions modules for all library materials, print and electronic. As new and developing platforms are designed to manage all library materials, they also include electronic resource management (ERM) services. With all library services as part of one system, platforms will be able to provide analytics for data in the system, including usage statistics for print and electronic materials, as well as reporting features for each of the services in the platform. Several new systems already include analytical dashboards for snapshot views of system statistics.

Discovery catalogs will also be an integral service of future library platforms. Already adopted by many libraries, these new public interfaces often function with external link resolvers and A-to-Z serial title lists for taking users from the catalog to full-text resources. Future systems will have all these components as part of the unified platform. In the platform, these public interface components will integrate with all other services, including authentication services governing access rights.

A single platform for all systems will allow for redesigned and combined workflows. Platform systems will be open so that one platform can use services from another if needed or desired, making use of web services and application programming interfaces (APIs). Systems will be built on service-oriented architecture (SOA), with individual yet connected functions, so that systems are scalable, or can be used by large and small operations to perform complex or simple services. Shared infrastructures will also incorporate shared and linked data sets and tools for analyzing system information and statistics. All this will allow for greater cooperation among libraries and a strengthening of patron-driven print and digital services, thus getting the information to the user and fulfilling her information needs.

CLOUD COMPUTING

In 1962 Ross Perot left IBM and started Electronic Data Systems (EDS), based around the idea that organizations with large mainframe computing hardware needed these systems only during business hours, and could lease afterhours processing time to other organizations. Though not widely credited as a founder of cloud computing, Perot's success demonstrates the idea that the computing needs of organizations are often lower than the capacity of the hardware they purchase. It is this inefficiency that has led to the recent explosion of cloud-based systems.

Since the mid-2000s the term *cloud* has been used to describe a wide range of services, from hosting providers who allow organizations to offload information technology (IT) infrastructure, to storage providers encouraging consumers to preserve data virtually. *The cloud* has come to mean a shared hardware environment with an optional software component.

While these services may describe cloud computing, they do not accurately describe the current state of cloud-based integrated library systems. Given the noncompetitive nature of most library environments, libraries have the unique opportunity to benefit from not only a shared hardware/software environment but also a shared data environment. A cloud-based ILS may best be understood as a shared system where all users benefit from the data contributions of participants.

These contributions can manifest themselves in a number of ways, from shared Machine-Readable Cataloging (MARC) records, to a shared online public access catalog (OPAC), where searches from all participating libraries enhance the relevancy ranking of results. It is this distinction that separates a cloud-based ILS from simply being a cloud-hosted ILS.

As a precursor to cloud computing, for several years there have been services providing access to software installations. At one time these services were referred to as the application service provider (ASP) model, now more commonly known as Software as a Service (SaaS). ASP/SaaS models have provided opportunities for organizations—including libraries—to access computing services and technology perhaps beyond the means of systems run in-house. Some organizations, although quite capable of running such infrastructures on premises, have been able to realize the cost savings of ASP/SaaS services: reduced infrastructures for technology, staffing, or both. Many organizations have become accustomed to relying on these provided services and have been able to shift resources to other areas of concentration within their work environment.

The use of cloud computing builds on the ASP/SaaS model and expands upon the opportunities for realized savings on reduced infrastructures. Cloud computing offers not only a hosted software and hardware infrastructure, but it provides means for accessing the software or related services online without any local installation of the software in question. The general Internet user is now accustomed to using services and software within the cloud by means of access via a standard web browser, although it may have taken somewhat longer to develop a formal understanding of the term *cloud computing*.

The discontinuance of the need for local software installation—and for separate software instances—is a substantial advantage of true cloud computing over the ASP/SaaS model. The ASP/SaaS model generally requires installation of software locally for access to a system. The infrastructure for the ASP/SaaS model is often still the same as a locally hosted system, but it is handled remotely by the service provider. Cloud-based computing is such that a single instance of a software system can be installed and run for access by many shared users, giving rise to a multitenant infrastructure, unlike the separate systems run in ASP/SaaS models. A shared-system environment running a single instance of a particular application is the basis for the creation of a platform. A platform is the foundation for a software environment with multiple related services and computing capabilities accessible within the cloud.

The multitenant shared infrastructure of a platform allows for quantifiable advantages. The service provider can spend time on development and quick implementation of new features and enhancements, as there is only one instance of the software to maintain. The reduced overhead for separate systems also allows the service provider to realize significant cost savings from not maintaining multiple separate infrastructures. This cost reduction must ultimately be at least partially realized by the libraries or other organizations using the provided software services.

It can be argued that open-source software has encouraged proprietary software vendors to create more open systems. This argument does not need to be made or supported. It is enough to note that now, and in the future, systems must be more open as the functionality of adopted and evolving web standards will require this. Open systems are relevant to cloud computing and platforms because not only are they contemporary developments, but they are essentially all made to work together. Web services provide means for extracting and using data from open systems, and the new platforms provided by cloud services are certainly systems from which data is sought.

Big data, linked data, and the analytics of this content are some of the advantages forthcoming from cloud computing. Libraries are finally realizing access to their own information that has for years been locked away in locally hosted, or at least discretely hosted, systems. Not only will libraries have better access to their data and statistics, the platforms of the cloud-based environment promise to offer better means for analyzing and using that information for creation of new business intelligence and enhanced service delivery.

SHARED TECHNOLOGICAL INFRASTRUCTURE

As can be expected, the model for future library systems has been developed in a broader realm than libraries, as this model is now prevalent among general IT operations. If cloud-based platforms are adopted in libraries, then multitenant architecture software—and the expectations for the provision of platform services in most current computing environments in general—will allow libraries to spend more time delivering services and less time running the systems they employ.

A platform will offer these systems as a package of cloud-based solutions. A shared cloud infrastructure has certain quantifiable and unquantifiable advantages over locally hosted and even individually external hosted systems. The cost savings of outsourcing software and hardware maintenance are measurable. It is in some ways immeasurable what libraries will gain by sharing future platform infrastructures, enabling the analysis of large-scale data sets (big data), along with individual library data that has previously been locked away in local systems, or not maintained by systems at all.

New library platforms will organize and maintain metadata as library systems have always done. By using shared-platform infrastructures, libraries will be able to take advantage of shared metadata within these systems. Bibliographic information will be open for shared use and enhancement, which will reduce duplicative work by eliminating the need to create local records for popular or widely held titles. This shared production environment will be enhanced by partnerships between libraries and other entities. Publishers and vendors are eager to share in the creation and enhancement of data sets, and libraries must become comfortable with allowing partnerships from varied organizations, including those from for-profit companies.

OPEN SYSTEMS AND LINKED DATA

Software systems within libraries and in other computing platforms are shifting from single-function, or single-system, designs, to service-oriented architecture (SOA). Computing services are individually running software functions that are linked to form a complex integrated system that can be seen as a whole consisting of interconnected separate operations. Developing and future library systems will use this newer architecture to connect all of the functions of library software to build the library platform.

A platform built on SOA is a scalable system— meaning that the functions of the system can be used by large-scale operations, or they can be scaled down to smaller implementations that maintain functionality and are meaningful in either environment. A large computing platform is designed to be scaled to need, and can grow to provide continuity in supporting operations. A powerful platform can also be used by a library with small or minimal system needs, as the infrastructure of the system is in the platform and need not be maintained by the individual libraries using the shared infrastructure.

Some libraries will opt to use a cloud-based system built with SOA but will not participate in a shared-platform environment. These systems, although in the cloud, will not be cloud-based in the sense of having a shared implementation; they will be open systems allowing for information exchange from one separate implementation to another. These connected systems will have the potential to connect services and make use of linked data.

The advent of linked data, as with linked systems, will allow for libraries to capitalize on the shared infrastructure of the actual data that is used to access information. In an environment where libraries are sharing bibliographic data, efforts can be made elsewhere, as duplication of work is minimized. Expanded access to bibliographic data as part of the Semantic Web will in fact allow libraries to have access to a much broader set of data, including data from any other entity that has linked data on the Internet. Of equal or greater importance, non-library entities will also be able to use library metadata if that metadata is part of the Semantic Web. This is essential as libraries work to become an included part of information retrieval on the Internet rather than isolated collections of locally accessible materials.

All this new interconnectedness for systems will enhance discovery of information materials, and will mean greater access to information for the user. Discovery systems, or next-generation OPAC replacements, are already using library metadata in new ways that allows the user to "discover" data through single-search interfaces and point-and-click access for refining searches. These search-refining parameters, or facets, are built from organized metadata that has been stored in the more closed integrated library systems of the past. Facets can provide information from multiple sources, including bibliographic records, item or holding records, and even vended data sources. In the future, these systems will become even more powerful as they incorporate linked data from other libraries and non-library resources alike.

NEW BIBLIOGRAPHIC FRAMEWORK

To sustain broader partnerships—and to be seen in the non-library specific realm of the Internet—metadata in future library systems will undoubtedly take on new and varied forms. It is essential that future library metadata be understood and open to general formats and technology standards that are used universally. Libraries should still define what data is gathered and what is essential for resource use, keeping in mind the specific needs of information access and discovery. However, the means of storage and structure for this metadata must not be proprietary to library systems. Use of the MARC standard format has locked down library bibliographic information. The format was useful in stand-alone systems for retrieval of holdings in separate libraries, but future library systems will employ non-library-specific formats enabling the discovery of library information by any other system desiring to access the information. We can expect library systems to ingest non-MARC formats such as Dublin Core; likewise, we can expect library discovery interfaces to expose metadata in formats such as Microdata and other Semantic Web formats that can be indexed by search engines.

Adoption of open cloud-based systems will allow library data and metadata to be accessible to non-library entities without special arrangements. Libraries spent decades creating and storing information that was only accessible, for the most part, to others within the same profession. Libraries have begun to make partnerships with other non-library entities to share metadata in formats that can be useful to those entities. OCLC has worked on partnerships with Google for programs such as Google Books, where provided library metadata can direct users back to libraries. ONIX for Books, the international standard for electronic distribution of publisher bibliographic data, has opened the exchange of metadata between publishers and libraries for the enhancements of records on both sides of the partnership. To have a presence in the web of information available on the Internet is the only means by which any data organization will survive in the future. Information access is increasingly done online, whether via computer, tablet, or mobile device. If library metadata does not exist where users are—on the Internet—then libraries do not exist to those users. Exchanging metadata with non-library entities on the Internet will allow libraries to be seen and used. In addition to adopting open systems, libraries will be able to collectively work on implementation of a planned new bibliographic framework when using library platforms. This new framework will be based on standards relevant to the web of linked data rather than standards proprietary to libraries.

The Library of Congress, with other partners, continues to work on a new bibliographic framework (BIBFRAME). This framework will be an open-storage format based on newer technology, such as XML. A framework is merely a holder of content, and a more open framework will allow for easier access to stored metadata. While resource description and access (RDA) is a movement to rewrite cataloging rules, BIBFRAME is a movement to develop a new storage medium. The new storage framework may still use RDA as a means of describing content metadata, but it will move storage away from MARC to a new format based on standardized non-library technology.

This new framework will encompass several important characteristics. It will transition storage of library metadata to an open format that is accessible for use by external systems, using standard technology employed outside of libraries. This will allow for libraries to share metadata with each other and with the rest of the Semantic Web. The new framework will also allow for the storage of both old and new metadata formats so that libraries may move forward without reworking existing records. Finally, the new framework will make use of formal metadata structure, as the benefit of named metadata fields has more power for search and discovery than the simple keyword searching employed by much of the Internet. Library metadata will become more important once its organized fields of information can be accessed by any standard non-library system.

Embracing a new storage format for bibliographic metadata is much like adoption of a new computer storage format, such as moving your data storage from CD-ROM to an external USB hard drive; the metadata that libraries have created for decades will not be lost but will be converted to a new, more accessible, storage format, sustaining access to the information. Although these benefits may be seen by some, it can be expected that there may be resistance to changes in format as well. It will be no small undertaking to define how libraries will move forward and to then provide means for libraries to transition to new formats. Whatever transitions may be adopted, it will be important that libraries not abandon a structured metadata entry form in lieu of complete keyword formatting.

Much of the Internet has been built on keyword searching for information retrieval, but there is continued value in defining what information is stored in specified metadata areas so that keyword searches can be better targeted. Areas or fields of metadata can be used for providing relevancy ranking for search results or specified searches (e.g., Author or Title), using a ranking system similar to other information sources such as websites. Using formats that are understood by those outside of libraries will make libraries more visible—sustaining libraries' relevance and increasing, enhancing, and enabling future development of new library services for the user.

ELECTRONIC RESOURCE MANAGEMENT AND EXPANDED ANALYTICS

Many libraries have already begun to acquire electronic materials into their collections. It is no longer relevant to the patron whether these resources are owned, leased, borrowed, or simply open access. Libraries focused on patron fulfillment—that is, meeting the information needs of the user—will continue to emphasize access to information in all its formats. Systems currently under development, and some already in use, are early attempts to incorporate management of all these types of resources. Systems will move from print-based management to new systems built with electronic resource management fully integrated with all functions of library operations.

Current electronic resource management (ERM) systems are often separate components of an integrated library system, and often have little interaction with other modules in an ILS. Although existing systems are not always part of an ILS, they have been built on standards including SUSHI (Standardized Usage Statistics Harvesting Initiative) and COUNTER (Counting Online Usage of Networked Electronic Resources). As future systems will fully incorporate electronic resources and their management, the usage statistics for those materials will be part of the growing data of information available in library platform systems.

Platforms will allow libraries to have a shared knowledge base of information. This shared knowledge base will allow for a shift in workflows. Electronic resources will be acquired and "turned on" from within services in the library software platform once a purchase decision is made. These materials will be instantly available in the system, which will already have defined access rights, holdings data, and other pertinent information maintained in the shared platform.

The knowledge base of a shared system will also allow for enhanced demand-driven acquisitions (DDA). Libraries will be able to offer access to materials by allowing the patron to make the purchase decision. Currently some systems allow for parameters or thresholds to be set so that a purchase is made for the user, or access to information is granted to the user on an at-need basis, instantly when the patron is searching. Systems can allow for brief access without a fee, or a purchase can be triggered after prolonged access or multiple views. Developing and future systems will allow for access to an unlimited collection of information that will grow as the user selects new materials for access. Access will then be limited only by the data contained in the knowledge base.

Along with DDA, cooperative collection development will be greater enabled through shared knowledge of what libraries already have access to. Libraries will be able to identify unique materials and avoid unnecessary collection overlap. Holdings information will be accessible in shared library platforms, as will be the usage information for those holdings, in both print and electronic formats.

Web services and APIs provide integrated library system users a means to access data over the Web using web-programming languages. This ability to extract and use library data in external systems has been described as open architecture, which is similar to open source. While *open source* indicates open access to source code, *open architecture* indicates open access to a system's data or functionality. Many libraries are already using APIs from discovery layer systems from various vendors to integrate article metadata into custom-created web applications. APIs for web-based systems will allow libraries to access library data for discovery, and will also enable functionality such as circulation, cataloging, electronic resource management, and statistical reporting.

Libraries will be empowered by library computing platforms with increased access to analytical data for holdings, usage statistics, and potentially user and other data in library platform systems. Each individual library not only will have greater access to its own information but will potentially be able to benchmark or compare data across multiple institutions. Platform systems, along with APIs and web services, will allow libraries to access their own information that was previously not accessible in closed integrated library systems. Most early platforms have limited reporting features, but future development is likely in this area as platform systems see greater use and new adopters define new reporting needs. Delivered analytical dashboards are already being designed to allow for custom display; these will include the option of custom reporting at a much greater level as systems continue to develop. Future reporting will include analysis of purchases, collections, and all other platform functions. Systems will be designed to meet the changing needs for analytical reporting, to keep pace with delivery of changing library services.

FOCUS ON FULFILLMENT AND ACCESS

For years, integrated library system models have served as disconnected, separate repositories of bibliographic metadata, in which both records and the work to create them have been often duplicated from library to library. The software and hardware for this model were separately maintained and financially sustained by each library using these systems. Consortia have arisen for sharing both physical and financial resources, but libraries are still disconnected in their daily operations, even within shared systems. New models will run on outsourced infrastructure, allowing efforts and finances to shift toward resource sharing and delivery of library user services.

If the original purpose of library science was to provide curated and organized access to information, the original purpose of integrated library systems grew out of the need to track a controlled inventory. The foundation of library services now— and in the future—is still to provide this access to information. System needs and designs, however, have shifted from inventory control systems to systems designed with the end purpose in mind: delivery of accessible information and fulfillment of the user's information access needs. This natural progression is imminent as libraries shift from curating owned, physical materials to providing access to print, electronic, and other format of materials from multiple collections that may or may not be owned or licensed by the library. Libraries are now being called to provide access to any information resource needed by the end user.

Integrated library systems developed around the premise of fulfillment will facilitate both traditional circulation and OpenURL access to electronic material. Cloud-based ILS will include metadata for journals, articles, and aggregators, along with a built-in link resolver providing a means to connect users to these resources. Libraries can then manage and assess electronic and physical usage within a single system.

Platforms will employ a multitenant architecture, allowing multiple libraries to use shared systems and services. This will, in turn, allow for the expanded provision of access to owned, leased, and borrowed information. Most patrons are not concerned with where the library gets materials, as long as the library is able to deliver access in a timely manner. The connected systems will allow for this expedited access to information, which the patron may already expect to be instantaneous. Security management for access will be part of some cloud-based ILS or linked from a combination of systems including the library platform.

WHAT LIES AHEAD?

In the next few years, there will be a proliferation of open architecture systems. By exposing library data through web protocols, types of access to library data will be endless; this increased portability will further encourage libraries to develop in-house discovery interfaces. These interfaces could then blend traditional MARC-born data with non-MARC metadata, merging traditional library resources with digital collections, institutional repositories, and research data sets. Juxtaposed, some cloud-based ILS may also focus heavily on discovery and will be built to ingest MARC and non-MARC metadata, allowing libraries to manage multiple types of data in a single interface.

The most promising aspect of this newfound portability will be the ability to crosswalk library data into linked data formats that search engines can then ingest and index. Whether developed in-house or by discovery-layer providers, new search engine optimized (SEO) ready search tools will bring users to library resources at the search engine level. SEO is the preparation of a website for search engines to index which then allows the content of a website to be findable within a search engine. Given the geolocation aspect of search engine relevancy—and regional nature of the library environment—matching a user to a resource via search engines will play a large role in future library systems.

Libraries embracing these technologies will look to create a new bibliographic framework focused on compatibility with linked data standards. These standards will enhance both search engine optimization and semantic searching. This new bibliographic format will open the library to new markets and has the potential to bring more users to library resources than ever before. Increased traffic from search engines may even curb downturns in circulation and increase lending between libraries. Increased lending and borrowing between libraries will have a cost, but this cost may actually be less than the cost of purchasing, processing, and storing new materials. Libraries will need to monitor changes in material usage, and to perform a cost/benefit analysis when entering these new environments.

This increased discovery of library resources will lead to an inevitable refocusing of library reference and instruction from navigating databases to evaluating resources. Libraries that continue to see declining reference statistics will likely realign staff into emerging fields such as digital publishing, digital preservation, data visualization, assessment, and scholarly communication. Ultimately, library patrons will benefit from enhanced discovery resulting from enhanced metadata.

The efficiencies brought about by cloud-based ILS will undoubtedly have their greatest impact on acquisitions and cataloging departments. Since these systems typically look to eliminate copy cataloging, libraries with special collections may look to reorganize technical services staff around original cataloging or digitizing collections. Libraries may also look to move catalogers into acquisitions or electronic resource management as demand dictates.

Library information technology operations adopting cloud-based ILS will also see changes in staffing needs. Since cloud-based ILS providers will handle hardware and software upgrades, library staff previously responsible for these tasks will have more time to participate in research and development of projects. These projects may involve integrating cloud-based ILS web services into current library web interfaces and assisting with assessment projects such as business intelligence applications.

Of all the changes resulting from migration to cloud-based ILS, the most significant will be libraries' expanded ability to develop new and innovative services. Libraries will have the opportunity to help solve more complex problems than ever before—and thus, patrons will be served with more library resources than ever before.

Library Discovery
From Ponds to Streams

Kenneth J. Varnum

Resource discovery in libraries has undergone a remarkable evolution over the past five years, tracking (but lagging behind) what has happened on the public Internet. As a handful of companies (Google, Bing, Yahoo!, Yandex, Baidu, etc.) have emerged to provide near-universal access to public information on the Internet, there has been a rising desire within the library world for similar access to licensed content. Libraries, and libraries' perceptions of the patrons' needs, have led to the creation and acquisition of "web-scale" discovery services. These new services seek to amalgamate all the content a library might provide access to—the catalog, online journals, abstracting and indexing databases, institutional repositories, open access sites, and more—into a single index. Much like the big companies on the public Internet, these new services build their indexes of content and provide access.

PRIMORDIAL DISCOVERY PONDS

The evolution of online library research has undergone a significant transformation as well. Not long ago, a library's online resource portfolio could be thought of as collection of ponds. While they might coexist in a broad ecosystem, they were only

A portion of this chapter is based on "Perspective on Discovery," which was published on RSS4Lib on September 26, 2013, www.rss4lib.com/2013/09/perspective-on-discovery/.

loosely connected closer to the surface (if at all). To conduct effective research, a library user would need to navigate to each pond in turn, dip his toes in (or dive in), but then would need to travel to another pond when investigations in the first were completed. Many scholars would find their particular favorite ponds and keep going back to them, regardless of how appropriate that particular collection of information was to the specific research problem at hand. For many users—particularly those who are deeply knowledgeable about their areas of study—this was an excellent tactic and served them well. These researchers often know the specific databases for their field. However, for researchers who are not experts in a field, or for those same experts who might be exploring the overlapping margins of two related disciplines, finding the right database, or series of databases, was onerous and often problematic. This feeling of inefficiency was strengthened by the rise of the Internet search engines that gave the appearance of total coverage.

To meet the desire for breadth of coverage, libraries turned to federated search technologies.[1] In a federated search, a single user query is directed to multiple databases simultaneously. A limited number of results from each database is retrieved and merged into a single result set. A number of vendors offered federated search products, including Ex Libris (Metalib), Millennium Access Plus (Innovative), and WebFeat's eponymous offering.

THE INFORMATION SEAS

Federated search moved the library patron from the pond to the ocean—or rather, allowed the searcher to more efficiently query multiple databases at once. In slightly more time than it took to get to and conduct a search in a single database, these tools searched multiple databases simultaneously and returned consolidated results from all of them. However, as significant an advance as federated searching was, it was beset by a host of challenges. A federated search is inherently slower than the slowest target database. This is because federated searching relies on a series of sequential processes. Once the search term is sent out to each target database, the search tool waits until results come back from all providers (or the response is "timed out" or otherwise fails to come back after some preset threshold of time). Because each database provides its own independent (usually proprietary) relevance ranking, the collected results then need to be reranked and presented in a consistent way. Until all this processing is done, the user sees either a "processing" message or an evolving results list where more relevant items supplant the ones already displayed on the screen.

Initially, this process was seen as a significant advance. However, as Internet search tools became faster and more all-encompassing, the user experience of federated search quickly began to pale. Library researchers became accustomed to the lightning-fast response times they would find when searching other online resources; the perception of a twenty- or thirty-second delay in a federated search product became intolerable. Patrons rarely were concerned about the fractured nature of back-end technologies that were being searched and integrated; if Google could do it, people reasoned, why can't the library?

OCEANS OF DATA

Despite these major challenges, federated search tools solved a need of many library patrons and libraries: they were a means of trawling the ocean of information available to them. And once they had seen the ocean, few wanted to return to the ponds. If federated search was not the solution, then perhaps the situation could be improved by taking a page out of Google's playbook and building a single index. These emerging tools combine the full text and indexing for hundreds of millions of scholarly objects into one huge index, which then can be searched in "Google time": quickly and efficiently, with a single relevance-ranking mechanism in effect, regardless of the source of the data.

Most discovery services provide a view of the entire collection of searchable information that is connected with the entitlements of the user who is doing the searching. The library provides its licensed content holdings to the discovery service, which then can mediate user queries against the corpus of material that is available to that user. Because the index includes a greater breadth of content than is available at any participating library, it is possible for a user query to be conducted against all content, not just content licensed for local access. Most libraries choose to limit the default search to readily available content but to allow the user to expand to the whole universe of materials.

Index-based discovery products for library content have a relatively brief history. Scholars Portal, a consortial effort in Ontario that brought together the physical and licensed collections of Ontario's twenty-one university libraries, pioneered the single-index approach for licensed library content in 2002.[2] Commercial products soon emerged from other sources, developed along the same conceptual lines. The first to reach the market was Serials Solutions' Summon service in 2009. Analogous products from EBSCO and Ex Libris were launched thereafter, joining OCLC's FirstSearch in this market area. While each tool has a different technological approach, the end effect for the library user is approximately similar: one search box that includes a broad selection—approaching totality—of content that approximates the library's owned and licensed digital content.[3]

In the four years since discovery services became commercially available, they have seen a rapid uptake by research libraries and, to a smaller degree, by public libraries. The concentration of discovery services in larger public libraries and academic libraries is due to two factors. The first, and far from trivial, is cost. These services tend to be expensive. The second factor is the breadth of content acquired by the library. Larger libraries tend to have more disparate data sources to search, with corresponding effort required by a researcher to be truly inclusive when looking for information. Smaller libraries often have smaller portfolios of licensed content and, often, acquire multiple databases from a single provider that already offers platform-wide searching. The need for integration is less keenly felt in these cases.

MOVING TO STREAMS

This brings us to the current stage, where many (mostly larger) libraries offer their patrons a Google-like experience: a single entry point to everything the library has to offer. Now that we have finally found the holy grail, we are beginning to understand that it comes with challenges of its own. In many use cases, library searchers indeed want—and need—access to the breadth of the library's holdings. They are doing truly exploratory searches and desire access to everything, or at least a representative sample. The increasing focus on interdisciplinary research highlights the benefits of searching the entire ocean of library content in one go. At the same time, many use cases indicate the advantage that a narrower scope provides, a simultaneously all-encompassing search of materials within subject disciplines, rather than across them.

Over the past decade—a time period that encompasses libraries' efforts to adapt to discovery tools—libraries have been finding ways to integrate their resources into their broader communities. This concept was defined by Lorcan Dempsey in 2005 in a well-known post, "In the Flow." He described a world in which the library should strive to make its services and resources available to researchers "in the user environment and not expect the user to find their way to the library environment," and in which the "integration of library resources [into other systems] should not be seen as an end in itself but as a means to better integration with the user environment, with workflow."[4] In the years since Dempsey wrote this, libraries have followed the course he described: embedding librarians in academic departments and research groups, making library-curated data available through open and automated mechanisms, integrating research tools into their websites, and more.

Dempsey's recommendation was that libraries place themselves in the flow of the research process. While being in the flow is essential, with current discovery technologies, libraries can now do more than make sure they are *in* the flow; we are now well positioned both to *create* streams of information that researches will dip into, and to provide functional and valuable access points to these streams. In many ways, this new capability to divert the oceans of information available through discovery systems into streams of context-appropriate resources for researchers, individually or collectively, will unlock the true value of resource discovery systems.

Streams, or flows, of information are not as useful if libraries do not tailor them to the specific categories of library users who will benefit most from accessing them. It is time for discovery to focus on the user interaction and experience, now that vast bodies of information are available to be searched.

I have long felt that discovery tools are most effective when they are presented in the context of the library whose patrons are doing the research. The discovery services' native interfaces are well designed, user tested, and largely accessible to users with varying degrees of print or physical ability, but they do not easily allow for mapping resources into categories that make sense at the local level. In an academic library setting, for example, it may well make sense to offer focused searches based on users' course enrollments. The University of Michigan library built an experimental tool several years ago to do just this.

In our experimental project, nicknamed "Project Lefty" (the goal was to get the user the right content, at the right level, in the right subject areas—and as we all know, three rights make a left), we developed a front end to our Summon system that scoped searches based on a user's course enrollment.[5] The system would take the user's search query and pass it on to the discovery tool, along with a set of resources (largely online journals, but the pool of resources could also include e-book collections or other full-text sources) that should be searched. A group of subject-specialist librarians organized journal titles relevant to their subject areas into one of three categories: novice, expert, or both. Journals in the novice category were those that were appropriate to lower-level undergraduate courses; generally, these were the more accessible peer-reviewed and popular journals in the subject area. Expert journals were the more narrowly focused, deeply scholarly publications. Some journals, of course, are broadly relevant to a subject area and were included in the "both" category. In terms of courses, we categorized 100-, 200-, and 300-level courses as "novice" and 400-level (and higher) as "expert."

Because we could ask campus users to log in to the system—and could therefore access basic course enrollment information about them—we could know which courses each student was enrolled in and present an option to focus a user search query on just those resources, identified by librarians, that were most likely to be appropriate for search query. For example, a student who was enrolled in a 100-level geology class, a 300-level economics class, and a 500-level psychology class could opt to apply her course filter to a search for *depression* and see, in turn, introductory materials on depression (the geographic feature), materials on depression (the economic condition), or deeply scholarly materials on depression (the psychological condition).

Conversely, such a system could allow a researcher to remove one's own native discipline from a results set. For example, a psychology scholar interested in the effects of the Great Depression on the mental health of the populace could search for *depression* but exclude economics content from the search results.

Discovery services offer a plenitude of keyword vocabularies, controlled and free-text, connected with the articles they index. Subject terms provided through controlled vocabularies or uncontrolled author association are rarely easy to distinguish, making pure keyword filtering a challenge. Having a focused title-based categorization is a more effective mechanism for scoping a search and allows libraries to bridge the gap between subject-specific databases and broad, source-agnostic discovery tools.

At a more generalized level, even if a library does not wish to provide purely individualized search results, an intermediate level is possible—a course-specific search interface that scopes the user's search to the materials determined to be most relevant. The same basic data categorization process would take place (though perhaps at a more granular level), through which subject specialists could assign course-level indicators to a range of online resources, taking into account course syllabi and the librarians' subject and content expertise. Course-specific searches would then cover this suite of resources. This would be of particular benefit to novice researchers who are getting familiar with the concepts of resource review and selection, by giving them simple, powerful interfaces into sets of resources that are germane to their needs.

AN UNTAPPED RESERVOIR

Much of the work around resource discovery up until now has been focused on the content being searched. The construction of large-scale single-index repositories of scholarly information has been a huge technical challenge. There have also been difficult negotiations with the publishers of full-text materials and the abstracting and indexing services that provide additional value and access points to the scholarly world through their contributions. The untapped input is the researcher. The next phase of discovery will focus on the consumer of the search results: the scholars, researchers, and library patrons in general. The researcher's identity carries with it a range of associated information that, if tapped on an individual basis, can streamline the research process. The researcher does not have to be only a consumer of the discovery service; the researcher can also be an input, transparently, to the search query.

This data is particularly accessible and relevant to academic libraries because they are generally well positioned to access the complete researcher ecosystem: information about students through campus directories and data from the registrar (courses enrolled in), information about faculty from institutional repositories (results of research already conducted) and the registrar (courses taught), along with campus directory information for everyone, and more. While equivalent data are possible to obtain in the public library context, the data sources are not as obvious and are much more likely to be sparsely provided through an opt-in system.

PRIVACY

Whether a system that treats "environmental" data about the researcher is opt-in or opt-out, it is important to remember that the system must be sensitive to the user's need for privacy and confidentiality. Libraries have the technical ability to access user-specific data to build personalized discovery environments, but should tap that reservoir only if there are ways for users to opt out on a permanent or case-by-case basis. Some researchers may not want to conduct a particular search through logging in; they may wish to remain anonymous throughout the process, and may not want to see tailored results ever. Other researchers may generally want to have access to tailored search results, but may want to step out of the personalized stream back into the ocean to see what they might be missing. Both needs are real and must be designed into whatever system is offered.

There is a strong argument to be made that these customizations are better done at the library level than by the vendor.[6] Libraries—and academic institutions— generally have more clearly articulated policies and procedures around information privacy than do vendors. It would be a difficult sell to pass along a user's course registration information to an external vendor, connected with a login, when the same information could be used on the library side of the relationship to tailor search results without exposing an individual user's identity to any vendor's system.

CONCLUDING THOUGHTS

The power of discovery, in my way of thinking, is not just in harnessing the local and the global—which is something in and of itself—but in providing tailored, focused access to that breadth. The value of discovery is much more than accessing the torrent of the Mississippi River as it dumps into the Gulf of Mexico. It is being able to tap into all the right tributaries out of the thousands that feed into the sea. Through careful use of user data and customizations (almost inevitably on the local side), libraries will be able to better serve their patrons in their quest for the right breadth and depth of information to meet their needs. The library of the near future will partake of communal data repositories, but do so in their own way.

NOTES

1. I will use *federated search* broadly, as a synonym for *metasearch*, ignoring the technical differences between the two. *Federated search* generally means searching across multiple databases at different network and physical locations, while *metasearch* generally means searching across multiple databases within a single network and physical location.

2. For more information, see "Scholars Portal: About," Ontario Council of University Libraries, http://spotdocs.scholarsportal.info/display/sp/About.

3. For more details on the discovery service landscape, see Marshall Breeding's library technology report, *Discovery Product Functionality* (ALA Editions, 2014).

4. Lorcan Dempsey, "In the Flow," June 24, 2005, *Lorcan Dempsey's Weblog,* http://orweblog.oclc.org/archives/000688.html.

5. See my article "Project Lefty: More Bang for the Search Query," www.infotoday.com/cilmag/apr10/Varnum.shtml, for a full description.

6. See Cody Hanson's 2013 presentation on "Why Web-Scale Means the End of Build vs. Buy" for more on what local interfaces can offer a library: www.slideshare.net/BaltimoreNISO/hanson-niso-nov-20-vc.

Exit as Strategy
Web Services as the New Websites for Many Libraries

Anson Parker, V. P. Nagraj, and David Moody

ALOHA

As you peruse these pages, know this: they have been penned by absolutely average developers. We're the grunts, followers of the Mack Truck Management Theory, and there are a lot of us out there.[1] So this is about sustainable development—we've stood on enough shoulders to know that ours can support a little weight. We offer you this chapter, which describes some of the work that we've done and why we think it matters. As you read this, you might see just how easy it can be to create web services and what opportunities they can bring to life.

Sundar Pichai, head of Android at Google, announced that the 2013 Google IO conference would focus on helping developers "write better things"—a shift from previous conferences that touted new products for consumers.[2] In the land of web development, this equates to creating web services: tools that allow other developers to gain access to our content stripped of all unnecessary layout and formatting. We're still delivering the "product" our "consumers" expect (i.e., a standard website), but as we open the door for other developers to interface with our content, we open the door for our content to appear elsewhere, and for our site to (dare to dream) cease to exist.

As librarians, we choose to adopt unifying standards to increase the interoperability and fluidity of our data. We frequently do not create the data itself; we reference it, catalog it, and make it as accessible as possible. Moving toward web services from websites is a natural progression for libraries. Take the example of the doctor looking at a patient record: in an ideal world, that patient record would automatically query a database of literature and show relevant results on the patient record—no search needed. Making triggers like this possible is the long-term goal of a web service. The example that follows in this chapter will be much more modest; however, it should help to explain some of the underlying technology of web services.

One of the earliest web services to hit the net was RSS. (While there are many flavors of RSS—including ATOM, RSS 2.0, etc.—we're going to discuss them all as RSS. For a more detailed breakdown of the similarities and differences, the Web offers many resources.[3]) Often dubbed "really simple syndication," RSS is a data transmission tool with a fixed schema with only a few—under twenty—fields, of which title, description, and URL are required. While RSS 2.0 and ATOM have enabled developers to extend this fixed schema by adding namespaces, most RSS readers do not incorporate this flexibility. Ultimately RSS works well for transmitting basic content; however, when passing robust structured content, it may not suffice. More descriptive data formats such as JSON exist to fill in this gap. JSON allows developers to create objects of unlimited size that may be given both a type (e.g. number, string, array) and a value (see figure 6.1).

Using JSON as a standard format, we show how to use several frameworks to create web services for developers while maintaining an effective product for end users. In our discussion, we focus on two frameworks: Drupal and Solr. Both Drupal and Solr are open-source, community-driven tools with corporate sponsorship and hundreds of thousands of enterprise-level constituents.

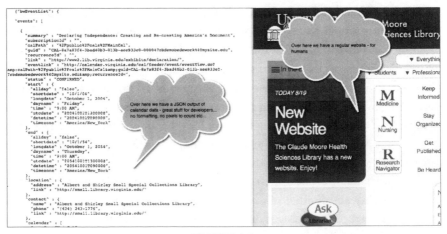

FIGURE 6.1
JSON and Rendered Web Page

Technology (Terms and Definitions)

Apache Solr. A popular search engine that we use to provide faceted searching of our site. It also is able to produce its responses as JSON, and it harvests objects in (among others) both RSS and JSON formats.

Drupal. A content management system (CMS) used by libraries and other enterprises around the world. It works with Solr and is capable of producing JSON and RSS feeds fairly simply.

GUID (globally unique identifier). A unique reference number used as an identifier, which can be helpful for keeping track of content that may otherwise seem identical.

JSON (JavaScript object notation). A data format capable of passing many types of structured content, and therefore offering more complete web services.

Piwik. An analytics tool that runs on our server and allows us to track exit pages of our patrons. Using trackback links, we are able to track use of our resources even when indexed and used through our web services.

Plone. Another CMS (like Drupal) that is in use at the University of Virginia Hospital for managing calendar events.

RSS (really simple syndication or rich site summary). A widely implemented but basic web service with a fixed number of fields. For simplicity's sake, we're using RSS as an umbrella for ATOM, RSS1, and RSS2 and using them rather interchangeably. While ATOM and RSS2 are extensible on the development side, it is uncommon to find readers who would take advantage of this; thus our decision to group them.

Solr as a web service. Provides developers with the power of the de facto standard open-source search and output formats of any imaginable type. Solr offers standard output formats out of the box that include JSON, XML, Python, PHP, and Ruby—a list that meets most any developer's data-digestion needs. Any other additional output requirements can be specifically met because Solr incorporates an XSLT response writer that captures the XML output and applies any transformation desired.

Web services. A family of tools involved in transmitting data stripped of formatting and layout requirements between domains.

XML (extensible markup language). A markup language that defines a set of rules for encoding documents in a format that is both human-readable and machine-readable. RSS is a subset of XML.

CHOOSING A WEB SERVICE STANDARD

Of the many technical religious wars, choosing a format for a web service is yet another. In many cases, this is a discussion to avoid, but in our use case we're going to need to look at the distinctions between formats a bit.

RSS is a great tool; there are millions (billions?) of RSS feeds out there, and the number keeps growing. RSS has a fixed (albeit evolving) schema.[4] A fixed schema in this case refers to the type of information that may be passed. For our example, let's imagine there's a new class being offered at the library that we want to feature as a calendar event (fig. 6.2).

```
<item>
<title>A Great Class</title>
<link>http://www.hsl.virginia.edu/events/index.cfm</link>
<guid isPermaLink="false">http://hsl.virginia.edu/1234</guid>
<description> A class for you!</description>
<pubDate>Wed, 21 Aug 2013 07:00:00 EST</pubDate>
<category>Library class</category>
</item>
```

FIGURE 6.2
A sample item from an RSS Feed

As a subset of XML, RSS adheres to familiar *<object>data</object>* markup. Here we have the required three fields (title, link, and description) as well as a publication date, a GUID, and a category. These values can be used to help filter content. All the tags in the RSS standard are fixed. This means you must call them exactly the same in all RSS feeds. So *<title>* must hold the title, *<link>* must have a link to the original content, and so forth.[5]

Now let's look at a JSON feed for the same kind of content (fig. 6.3).

With a JSON feed we are now seeing dozens of terms matched to their content in a *key:value* pairing system. There is also a hierarchy to the notation, such that *"location"* now has the attributes *"address"* and *"link"* because it is a subset of the overall *"events"* key. The JSON format may be extended indefinitely, and there are no required fields as in RSS. The advantage of this is clear: with JSON you may describe your structured data to the degree you are willing to type. The cost of this descriptive capability is that the developer on the receiving end must address the various fields and hierarchies (see fig. 6.4).

```
{
  "bwEventList":{
  "events":[
  {
  "summary":"A Great Class",
  "guid":"CAL-8a7a83f4-3bad40b3",
  "eventlink":"http://www.hsl.virginia.edu/events/index.cfm",
  "start":{
  "longdate":"October 1, 2013",
  "dayname":"Friday",
  "time":"9:00 AM"
  },
  "end":{
  "longdate":"October 1, 2013",
  "dayname":"Friday",
  "time":"10:00 AM"
  },
  "location":{
  "address":"Our Library",
  "link":"http://hsl.virginia.edu/map"
  },
  "contact":{
  "name":"A great librarian",
  "phone":"(434) 555-1212"
  },
  "categories":[
  "tag/Ongoing Excitement",
  "Tags",
  "Classes"
  ],
  "description":"This is a great class.",
  "cost":"FREE"
  }
  ]
  }
}
```

FIGURE 6.3
A sample item from a JSON Feed

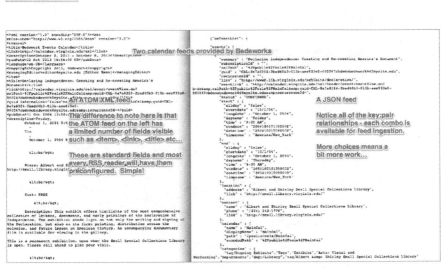

FIGURE 6.4
Sample Calendar Feeds

IN PRACTICE

Working with the UVa Calendaring Systems

Our first practical application of a web-services approach stemmed from a need for event listings on our website. The Claude Moore Health Sciences Library is in a strange position—we exist as an appendage of the University of Virginia, but are more firmly tied to the UVa Health System. Both entities have distinct calendaring systems. Because the library aspires to facilitate collaboration across campus, we aimed to mingle the interests of both of these constituencies while populating calendar data. In doing so, we could also highlight classes, exhibits, and other events happening in the library. The goal was simple—exposure:

- Expose university-wide events to Health System stakeholders.
- Expose library events to a university-wide audience.
- Expose library events to Health System stakeholders.
- Expose augmented calendar data to developers.

The UVa calendar is built with Bedework, an open-source calendaring product (www.jasig.org/bedework). It conforms to current calendar standards and offers a clean and approachable interface for listing events. We decided to input library event listings directly into this system rather than merge objects later—we could push data in, and then dynamically pull it back to our site.

The ease of data entry is matched by the flexibility of data output. The calendar offers feeds in a variety of data formats: RSS, ICS (iCalendar), XML, or JSON. We chose JSON. This tool is highly configurable—we can facet event listings based on categories that are appropriate to our patrons. Our feed excludes listings that may be irrelevant but includes events that are not listed on the Health System calendar. Slavic Languages & Literatures? We probably don't need that. Computer Science? Yeah, that might be relevant to Health System stakeholders, but wouldn't be listed on the Health System calendar. Once we are done faceting, we pull library events (along with those corresponding to the categories we selected) into Drupal. All this data will be merged and indexed with event listings pulled from the Health System calendar.

Unlike the central UVa calendaring tool, the Health System calendar was built in Plone (http://plone.org). This presents some limitations, chiefly that the event listings are only available via RSS 1.0 feed. We discussed above why this isn't ideal. In this case, we get fewer fields, which means less description and more work for us post-ingest. We can map and manipulate the data from the feed so that it can be indexed just as effectively as the main UVa event listings. With the Health System data in Drupal alongside the events from the central UVa feed, we can merge the content and display it on our site as a calendar. Once merged, we are able to index all the calendar items with Solr, which cleans up the data and makes events discoverable on our site via basic search.

Solr was introduced in 2004 as part of CNET's search strategy.[6] In 2006 it was open sourced, and today it is used by millions of people daily. Now it is one of the most widely used open-source search engines in the world, and has been implemented by enterprises such as Netflix, Zappos, and the United States government. Solr is capable of indexing many different kinds of objects—everything from websites to maps to solar systems. Solr's facility in relating and recommending content makes it especially attractive for our calendar data. A patron searching for an event could discover other events, pages, or users that are related to that event. Solr has also been recognized for its nimble interaction with Drupal, our CMS of choice.

Faceting, ingesting, mapping, manipulating, indexing—all of this amounts to added value for the patrons who use our calendar. That value proliferates beyond the end user, and it does so because we provide web services. We make our data available as JSON and RSS for developers to improve and repurpose. Our content works for us, but one could imagine different use cases for the same data. We'll leave that for the developers who have those use cases. But we'll give them a

73

hand along the way. Using Drupal, we can configure and adjust the output of our content with a high degree of granularity. Solr can also output results in a myriad of formats, including JSON, XML, RDF, Python (objects), PHP (objects), and Ruby (objects). We choose to provide data in both JSON and RSS format. We consider this redundancy an important feature; although we support JSON as a standard, we strive to make our data as usable as possible, and we understand that other calendaring tools may only support ingest of RSS content.

This is all described abstractly. What we'll do next is walk you through each step, each setting, and each button that we push to make this happen.

The Workflow: A Step-by-Step JSON Walkthrough with Drupal and Solr

1. Someone enters a calendar event in Bedework, Plone, or where-have-you. Once the calendar entry is completed, Bedework allows XML, RSS, iCal, and JSON formats for exporting the content.

2. In Drupal parlance we must now create a "content type" to store this content locally. This container will serve for all our event content that we are harvesting. Content types serve as structured containers for data. As we ingest the calendar data that we entered elsewhere, Drupal will create individual nodes of the "Event" content type for each event. It's worth noting that if for some reason a librarian wants to list an event only on our site and not on the main calendar site, that too is an option. The container exists, and content may be added manually or through feeds. See figure 6.5 for the result of a created content type.

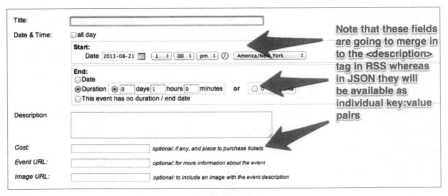

FIGURE 6.5
Calendar Item Data Entry Screen

3. Because we've already added our content to the main university calendar, we want to avoid double data entry. We'll use the Feeds module to help us in this process. Feeds is a tool in Drupal that is designed to harvest content in many formats: XML, JSON, RSS, CSV, and even direct SQL harvesting (provided you have credentials to the given database).[7] Feeds then auto-populates the content type based on field mappings that you establish.

4. Because RSS has a fixed schema, importing RSS feeds is a very straightforward process (see figure 6.6).

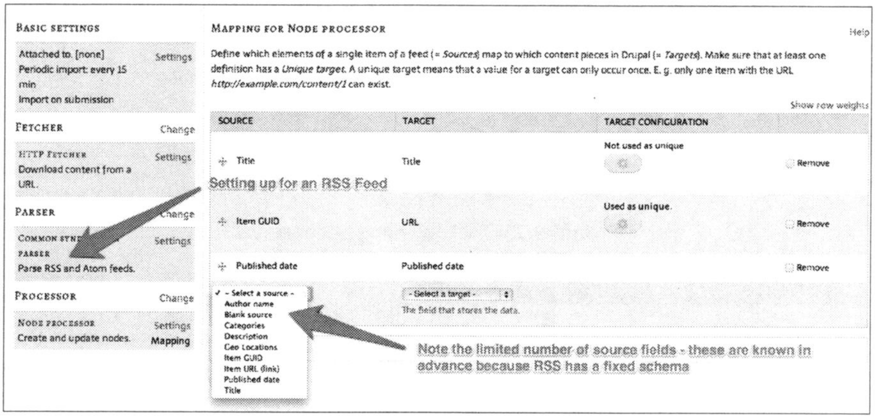

FIGURE 6.6
Setting up an RSS Feed

5. Creating a mapping with JSON requires two steps (see figures 6.7 and 6.8). In this example we declare the main context as "$.bwEventList.events.*" (with the asterisk here used as a wildcard to include all the content within the context), and after that we parse the rest of the JSON feed using the key values with periods used to go deeper in the hierarchy. For expedience we defined our context-two levels into the JSON document. *bwEventList* is the top level of our document, and under that is the events key. We might just as easily have specified the context as $.* and then defined each mapping, such as *bwEventList .events.events.location.address*, for instance. But by defining the context-two layers deep at the top, we've saved ourselves a few keystrokes.

6. Now that we've pulled our RSS and JSON feeds into Drupal, we're about halfway there. We've enjoyed two other sites' web services, and now it's time for us to create our own web service. While creating web services we'll also give our patrons something to see. The patron perspective for our calendar data may

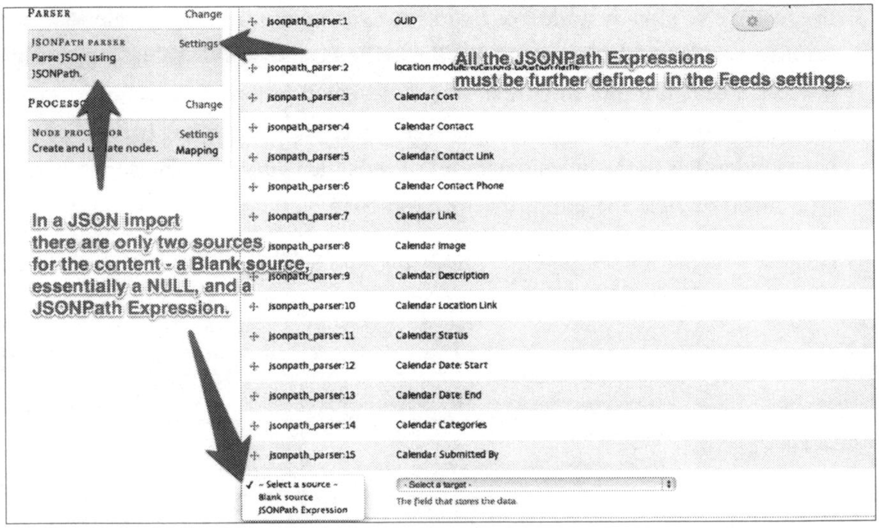

PARSER Change

JSONPATH PARSER Settings
Parse JSON using
JSONPath.

PROCESSOR Change

NODE PROCESSOR Settings
Create and update nodes. Mapping

In a JSON import
there are only two sources
for the content - a Blank source,
essentially a NULL, and a
JSONPath Expression.

+ jsonpath_parser:1 GUID

+ jsonpath_parser:2 location module...

All the JSONPath Expressions
must be further defined in the Feeds settings.

+ jsonpath_parser:3 Calendar Cost
+ jsonpath_parser:4 Calendar Contact
+ jsonpath_parser:5 Calendar Contact Link
+ jsonpath_parser:6 Calendar Contact Phone
+ jsonpath_parser:7 Calendar Link
+ jsonpath_parser:8 Calendar Image
+ jsonpath_parser:9 Calendar Description
+ jsonpath_parser:10 Calendar Location Link
+ jsonpath_parser:11 Calendar Status
+ jsonpath_parser:12 Calendar Date: Start
+ jsonpath_parser:13 Calendar Date: End
+ jsonpath_parser:14 Calendar Categories
+ jsonpath_parser:15 Calendar Submitted By

✓ – Select a source –
Blank source
JSONPath Expression

– Select a target –
The field that stores the data.

FIGURE 6.7
Initial JSON Mapping Screen

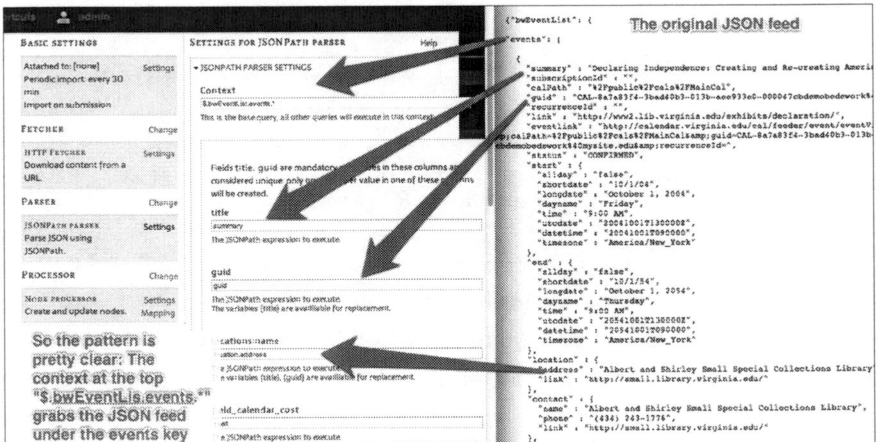

BASIC SETTINGS

Attached to: [none] Settings
Periodic import: every 30
min
Import on submission

FETCHER Change

HTTP FETCHER Settings
Download content from a
URL.

PARSER Change

JSONPATH PARSER Settings
Parse JSON using
JSONPath.

PROCESSOR Change

NODE PROCESSOR Settings
Create and update nodes. Mapping

So the pattern is
pretty clear: The
context at the top
"$.bwEventLis.events.*"
grabs the JSON feed
under the events key

SETTINGS FOR JSONPATH PARSER Help

▾ JSONPATH PARSER SETTINGS

Context
$.bwEventList.events.*

This is the base query, all other queries will execute in this context.

Fields title, guid are mandatory ... in these columns ...
considered unique only ... value in one of these ...
will be created.

title
summary
The JSONPath expression to execute.

guid
guid
The JSONPath expression to execute.
The variables [title], [guid] are available for replacement.

...cations:name
...ation:address
a JSONPath expression to execute...
variables [title], [guid] are available for replacement.

...ld_calendar_cost
...et
JSONPath expression to execute.
...re variables [title], [guid], [locations:name] are available for replacement.

{"bwEventList": { The original JSON feed
"events": [{
"summary" : "Declaring Independence: Creating and Re-creating Ameri
"subscriptionId" : "",
"calPath" : "%2Fpublic%2FMainCal",
"guid" : "CAL-8a7a83f4-3bad40b3-013b-aee933e0-00004?cbdemobodework%
recurrenceId" : "",
"link" : "http://www2.lib.virginia.edu/exhibits/declaration/",
"eventlink" : "http://calendar.virginia.edu/cal/feeder/event/eventV
...calPath=%2Fpublic%2Fcal%2FMainCal&guid=CAL-8a7a83f4-3bad40b3-013b
...mdemobodework%40mysite.edu&recurrenceId=^,
"status" : "CONFIRMED",
"start" : {
"allday" : "false",
"shortdate" : "10/1/04",
"longdate" : "October 1, 2004",
"dayname" : "Friday",
"time" : "9:00 AM",
"utcdate" : "20041001T130000Z",
"datetime" : "20041001T090000",
"timezone" : "America/New_York"
},
"end" : {
"allday" : "false",
"shortdate" : "10/1/54",
"longdate" : "October 1, 2054",
"dayname" : "Thursday",
"time" : "9:00 AM",
"utcdate" : "20541001T130000Z",
"datetime" : "20541001T090000",
"timezone" : "America/New_York"
},
"location" : {
"address" : "Albert and Shirley Small Special Collections Library",
"link" : "http://small.library.virginia.edu/^"
},
"contact" : {
"name" : "Albert and Shirley Small Special Collections Library",
"phone" : "(434) 243-1776",
"link" : "http://small.library.virginia.edu/^"
},
"calendar" : {

FIGURE 6.8
JSON Mapping Screen after Declaring the Mappings

be presented a number of ways. Views is a popular way to display content in Drupal (see figure 6.9 for an example). Much like feeds, there are many ways to extend Views (http://drupal.org/project/views).

7. The first view we create will be a tabled page of all our events listed sorted by date. Because the Bedework calendar has a JSON output, we are able—without any manual labor—to extract start and end dates.

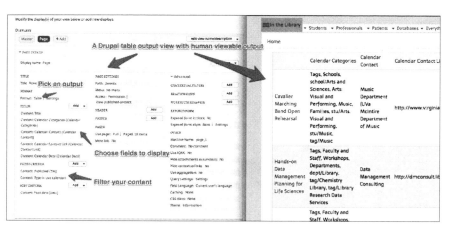

FIGURE 6.9
Comparing Views Settings and Rendered Output

For [All displays ▼]

Root object name
[nodes]
The name of the root object in the JSON document. e.g nodes or users or forum_posts

Top-level child object
[node]
The name of each top-level child object in the JSON document. e.g node or user or forum_post

Field output
⦿ Normal
◯ Raw
For each row in the view, fields can be output as either the field rendered by Views, or by the raw content of the field.

☑ Plaintext output
For each row in the view, strip all markup from the field output.

☐ Remove newlines
Strip newline characters from the field output.

JSON data format
⦿ Simple
◯ MIT Simile/Exhibit
◯ To be consumed by jqGrid
What object format will be used for JSON output.

Some basic settings for JSON or JSONp output

JSONP prefix
[ ]

If used the JSON output will be enclosed with parentheses and prefixed by this label, as in the JSONP format.

FIGURE 6.10
Views Settings to Configure JSON Output

8. Views Data Source (http://drupal.org/project/views_datasource) is a helper module for Views that will allow you to output content in JSON, XML, and so on. Now that we've ingested all of this content, we can spit out the aggregated Health System and UVa calendars as either RSS or JSON feeds and be done with it (see figures 6.10 and 6.11). We've now gone full circle—from JSON and RSS,

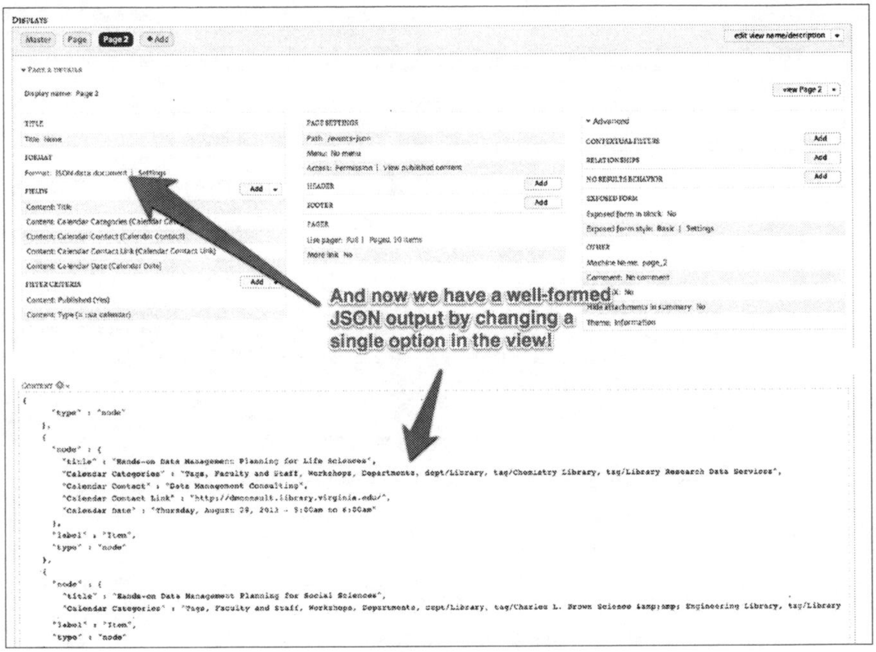

FIGURE 6.11
Sample JSON Output

to human viewable display, and back out as JSON and RSS for other complete strangers to devour and regurgitate as their own web services.

Indexing in Solr: What If We Could Do More?

Indexing content with SOLR is a technical and meticulous process (see figure 6.12). The ApacheSolr module in Drupal (http://drupal.org/project/apachesolr) takes care of most of the complexity for us. To index content with this tool, go to administration "Configuration" > "ApacheSolr Search" > "Default Index" tab. Here you can easily check the content types like the events we created earlier in the chapter to add to your Solr index, as in figure 6.13. Much as we have done with our Views, we are aiming to create both patron and developer tools.

For the Patron

For the patron we need do little more than turn on the Solr and Drupal. The defaults work off the shelf with little need to adjust anything. Search results are displayed with facets if desired, and the net result looks a lot like figure 6.14.

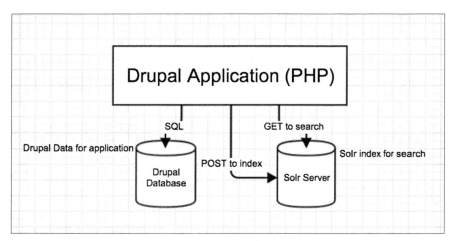

FIGURE 6.12
Schematic of Site Architecture

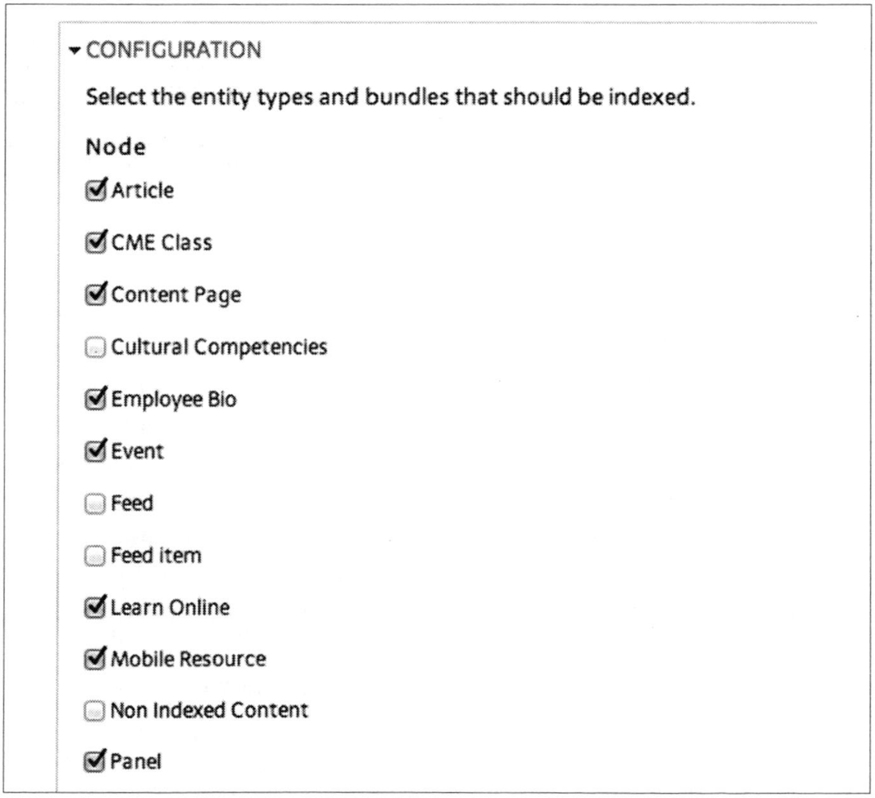

▼ CONFIGURATION

Select the entity types and bundles that should be indexed.

Node

☑ Article

☑ CME Class

☑ Content Page

☐ Cultural Competencies

☑ Employee Bio

☑ Event

☐ Feed

☐ Feed item

☑ Learn Online

☑ Mobile Resource

☐ Non Indexed Content

☑ Panel

FIGURE 6.13
Configuring Solr in Drupal

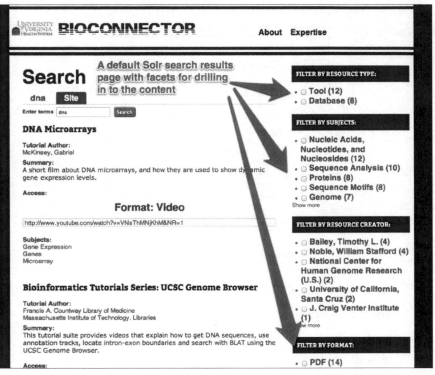

FIGURE 6.14
Sample Faceted Solr Search Results in Drupal

For the Developers

Now that we've got the 99 percent of our users taken care of, it's time to make work lighter for the developer community. Solr provides search results in many formats, including JSON. This data may be used by our development team or exposed to any developer. Retrieving the JSON data is easy. Because Solr searches are made and retrieved through a simple URL or REST (representational state transfer) request, you can simply add a *"wt=JSON"* parameter to your Solr search REST URL to give you the output in JSON format. Your search URL will look something like this:

```
http://yourdomain.com:8983/solr/your-collection/select?q=
*your-search*&wt-json
```

After receiving the JSON data in your REST response, you can now use it in your applications however you want.

One consideration for exposing your Solr data is for client-side application work. It is worth mentioning that Solr can help you get around the JSON cross-domain browser security issues by also exposing the data is a slightly modified JSON format, JSONP. This means that, for instance, if Virginia.edu wants to pull services from Yale.edu, it's entirely possible.[8]

To obtain the JSONP format, simply add *"json.wrf=callback"* to your REST URL. It will now look something like

```
http://yourdomain.com:8983/solr/your-collection/select?q=
*your-search*&wt-json&json.wrf=callback
```

By using the JSONP format your new application will not throw the errors associated with using content generated from a domain other than the destination URL.

81

MEASURING SUCCESS

We do a pretty good job keeping tabs on how our library's website is being used. Google Analytics gives us all kinds of metrics—we know (roughly) who is using what when, where, and how. But in the world we're advocating, websites take a backseat to web services. We're offering our data by various means in various formats to be reused by various entities for various purposes. How do we keep track? A standard tool like Google Analytics won't cut it off the shelf. How do we measure success in this paradigm?

It's a serious question, and we don't have a final answer. We're experimenting with some resources that are beginning to help us track usage. One of these tools is Piwik; it does a good job of monitoring activity. Because it's run on the server, it is able to track all URLs from the Apache logs, rather than working (as Google Analytics does) by inserting a tracking code on every page. This means that the views that are being used to create JSON feeds are quantifiable. Another tool we can use to measure the implementation of our web services is the Apache Solr Stats module (https://drupal.org/project/apachesolr_stats), with the results as seen in figure 6.15. Solr also provides statistics from its administrative panel, which has become much more robust as of the 4.x release. While these tools certainly give us a better sense of how developers may be using our tools, we are still looking for better ways to monitor.

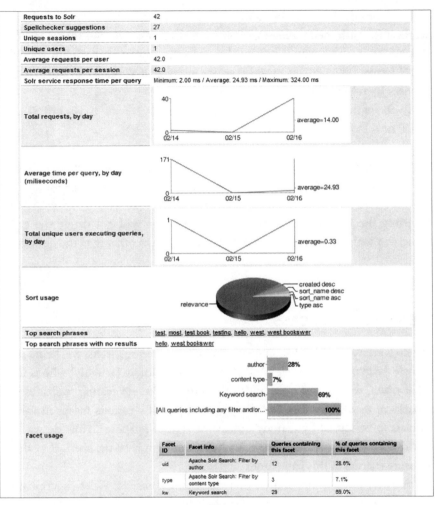

Requests to Solr	42
Spelichecker suggestions	27
Unique sessions	1
Unique users	1
Average requests per user	42.0
Average requests per session	42.0
Solr service response time per query	Minimum: 2.00 ms / Average: 24.93 ms / Maximum: 324.00 ms

82

FIGURE 6.15
Solr Usage Statistics

MOVING FORWARD

We know that the scope of our use case might obscure the bigger picture. Our implementation of web services is admittedly humble. We're talking about calendar data—so what? To really discuss the implications of this approach, we have to take a few steps back and look at the broader environment of what is happening in academic libraries.

Today users of information systems have choices, and libraries are desperately trying to stay relevant. One approach to advocating library services is to embed librarians in domain-specific contexts. The embedded librarian has become a familiar role in academic libraries.[9] In this paradigm, the library goes to the patron rather than the other way around. A web-services approach mirrors this shift by taking resources straight to the dashboards of third-party software.

But if we are embedding our data in other systems, then why should users come to the library website at all? Our answer: maybe they shouldn't. We have to be realistic about how our patrons look for information. If we are so conceited as to believe that our website should be the only space for our resources, then we close ourselves off from a whole group of users and a whole suite of services we could provide. By increasing access points for library data, we increase the access points for library services.

Let's go back to the example of the doctor looking at the patient record: this is a physician who may not have the time or inclination to seek out library services. But if we make our collections data available to the EMR (electronic medical record) software, then he can still benefit from relevant resources he serendipitously discovers. These have been described and curated by librarians, who also serve as a point of contact for training and instruction. At no point has he navigated to the library website—we have to be okay with that.

So will the library of the future even have a website? It isn't likely we'll shutter our doors or our website any time soon. But as developers move to adopt techniques that integrate their data with other systems, library websites may be more austere than they are today. Accepting this outcome is the biggest challenge to implementing a web-services approach. As we've shown, technical frameworks such as Drupal and Solr can help developers efficiently create robust, scalable web services. And while tools exist to monitor nontraditional metrics of web-services implementations, politically justifying this shift can be a tall order. So it might be a few years before the dashboards our patrons use are tightly integrated with the resources available in our institution—but when the political dust settles, we'll be ready.

ACKNOWLEDGEMENT

We would like to send a special thanks to Vincent Massaro of Yale University for getting us started with the Feeds JSON Calendar work.

NOTES

1. "Knowledge Hoarders & the Mack Truck Theory," accessed March 13, 2014, http://askthemanager.com/2008/07/knowledge-hoarders-the-mack-truck-theory/.

2. Steven Levy, "New Android Boss Finally Reveals Plans for World's Most Popular Mobile OS," *Wired*, May 13, 2013, www.wired.com/business/2013/05/exclusive-sundar-pichai-reveals-his-plans-for-android/.

3. See Fred Oiveira's "RSS vs. Atom, You Know, 'For Dummies,'" http://blog.webreakstuff.com/2005/07/rss-vs-atom-you-know-for-dummies/, and Ben Joan's "Difference between RSS and ATOM," www.differencebetween.net/technology/difference-between-rss-and-atom/.

4. Dave Winer, "RSS 2.0 at Harvard Law," the Berkman Center for Internet & Society at Harvard Law School, July 15, 2003, http://cyber.law.harvard.edu/rss/rss.html.

5. RSS 2.0 and ATOM formats are extensible; however, they require the user to add namespaces to the RSS feed. While this is not necessarily difficult, it requires the developer to delve in to namespaces to find their desired extension. Also worth noting: the average feed reader is going to ignore most of this information, so for the developer, JSON becomes an attractive solution.

6. Wikipedia, sv. "Apache Solr," accessed March 13, 2014, http://en.wikipedia.org/wiki/Apache_Solr.

7. Relevant Drupal modules include Feeds XPath Parser (https://drupal.org/project/feeds_xpathparser), Feeds JSONPath Parser (https://drupal.org/project/feeds_jsonpath_parser), and Feeds SQL (https://drupal.org/project/feeds_sql).

8. If you have this need, the following two resources will help you understand this slight but necessary data variation: Wikipedia's article on JSONP (http://en.wikipedia.org/wiki/JSONP) and skipperkongen's article "SOLR with JSONP with JQUERY" (http://skipperkongen.dk/2011/01/11/solr-with-jsonp-with-jquery/).

9. K. Brady and M. Kraft, "Embedded & Clinical Librarianship: Administrative Support for Vital New Roles," *Journal of Library Administration* 52, no. 8 (November 2012), 716–730.

Reading and Non-Reading
Text Mining in Critical Practice

Devin Higgins

As information takes new forms, new attitudes toward it develop in tandem. The arrival of digital text has allowed us to imagine interacting with the printed word in new, distinctly digital ways. It has become possible to "do" more with digital text collections than was ever remotely possible with their physically printed counterparts. As all readers are surely aware, the arrival of digital text has brought monumental changes in how we access text, both in the case of books—many of which are now accessible from potentially anywhere in the world—and also in terms of specific textual content on the level of individual words, which now may be plucked from the seas of language that surround them by the simple use of the now-ubiquitous search function. Almost now quaint in technologists' terms, the search bar has transformed our means of access to individual words or passages that in their printed form were hidden within piles of pages that could only be scanned for meaning by eye or by touch. Reading text online and using search functions are fundamental features of our digital culture, and have been absorbed by most all casual readers.

But the affordances of digital text today go much further. Scholarly researchers, particularly those in the humanities at the current moment, are increasingly reckoning with more rigorously digital approaches to exploring, processing, and transforming digital text. The loose set of practices called "text mining" or "text analysis," along with their close cousin "data mining," have allowed researchers to approach text in new ways, to "test" claims that were previously untestable (certain types of literary-historical arguments, for instance), to expand the scale at which literary work can be done—work that was previously limited by time and a scholar's powers of memory—and to encourage fresh perspectives on text at all scales; more on each of these below.

Though text mining is still (and perhaps always will be, pending developments in artificial intelligence) impossibly far from replacing that ideal of close human attention to linguistic information we usually call "reading," the inert printed words on a page that comprise a book can come to seem, even as we are reading them, very distant and inaccessible in certain key ways. Though the stream of sentences on page or screen may be perfectly available to reading or other sense-based examination, the material features of the text (its properties of length, number, distance, or of part of speech on a large scale) do not emerge to the human sensorium in any easy way. No single memory is capable of retaining mental word counts or statistically significant word co-occurrences for even one book-length text, let alone for the massive corpora available today for study by linguists and other scholars. Digital texts allow language content to become more like "data"; that is, something that can be processed computationally to reveal anew the brute properties of the text, and then manipulated in analytical and creative ways. Such properties on their own might have nothing to do with the meaning of the text, yet with the help of scholarly interpretation, they can generate new forms of understanding relevant to literature, music, the fine arts, or other areas of inquiry previously thought to occupy terrain a safe distance from the world of data and its methods.

In a recent blog post, Ted Underwood remarked astutely that "data mining is troubling for some of the same reasons that social science in general is troubling. It suggests that our actions are legible from a perspective that we don't immediately possess, and reveal things we haven't consciously chosen to reveal."[1] Text mining remains foreign and distant from us, on some level, because it operates using methods that bring out features of text that were always there but "illegible" to us as human readers. One is reminded of Emile Durkheim's classic sociological text *Suicide*, an explication of the phenomenon that looks to exhaustive sets of demographic data about those who commit suicide, rather than seeking explanatory meaning in notes left behind or other directly personal, psychological evidence.[2] The impersonal population-level data provides the basis for a different kind of meaning. Thus suicide was brought into a social understanding, through methods that existed outside of an immediate human perspective.

Text mining similarly provides a highly—or, at least, *differently*—mediated version of the materials on which it works, deriving information that is arguably directly factual about the content of the text under examination, yet that also alienates us from the *meaning* of the text as we know it. The machine-aided analysis of text is useful precisely because it partially and temporarily divorces the text from our own human response to it, showing us facets of it we never would have discovered independently, either because of the limitations to our faculties of memory and stamina, or because of culturally derived expectations systematically leading us in other directions. We have, after all, been trained to read and interpret. Yet to forge meaningful conclusions from text-mined data, it is necessary, ultimately, to incorporate these methods that expose text to us in new ways into some kind of an interpretive framework that renders this data meaningful. The data is not an argument in itself, rather the basis for one.

Text-mining techniques are particularly valuable when dealing not with individual documents, but with larger masses of text as *corpora* that can be queried and "read" in new ways, along the lines, for instance, of what Franco Moretti termed "distant reading."[3] The field of world literature is impossibly large and diverse, far too large to be read closely in its entirety. As Moretti points out, because it's not possible to read everything, or even a significant subset of everything, then it would be helpful to have a means of accessing, and, one hopes, making meaning from, that which remains unread. The text mining toolbox can offer the scholar of text the super-human capacity to engage *on some level* with thousands of texts at once, and to draw out information that otherwise would have required a lifetime of work, not to mention amazingly prodigious powers of memory and critical acumen.

TEXT MINING IN PRACTICE

Corpora linguistics is a well-established subfield that uses bodies of text (up to billions of words) to understand language-usage patterns on an unheard-of scale. The popular Google n-grams tool (http://books.google.com/ngrams) allows users to quickly and easily view how word usages have fluctuated over time, or blipped in and out of existence. There are now roughly half a billion words (or more precisely, word tokens) from twenty million volumes backing these results. Google invites one to view, as an example, how the trajectories of the words *hippie*, *flapper*, and *yuppie* have played out over time.[4] Without digital text, linguists could have made strong claims about the usage of these words across the last century, based both on common sense and on a set of historical or sociolinguistic suppositions developed by their field over time; but the n-grams tool provides a way to directly access the fluctuating word usages that partially undergird these suppositions. The n-grams tool is a way to test out hunches, assumptions, or even received wisdom. The work of linguists is still to describe the change revealed in the data, and make a case for its meaning in linguistic, social, or other terms.

Similar techniques are becoming increasingly popular throughout the humanities, not without some degree of controversy. The rise of text mining as a valid scholarly method, and of the digital humanities generally as an approach or area of inquiry, is vexing to many scholars for a variety of reasons, including that expressed in the view that "textual research belongs in current humanities departments only as a 'service' activity, not fully integrated in or related to the loftier philosophical aspirations of postformalist humanities."[5] This viewpoint expresses quite rightly that text mining need not be considered "lofty" in itself, but underestimates the value that text-based digital techniques might contribute to scholarship. Text mining can very well be an ingredient in lofty philosophizing, in the same way that close reading might. The role of text mining as a means not an end in humanities research would seem to be a prerequisite for integrating its methods into humanities departments more effectively.

Another criticism stems from the thought that the digital humanities represent an existential threat to the methods employed by humanists for centuries. Again, though, the bare results of computational text processing are wholly unpersuasive as critical arguments in themselves (if still possibly interesting and useful as data) without those same methods of research, close reading, and interpretation that humanists still use in conventional scholarly work. Regardless of information source, interpretive techniques are still needed to make sense of the mounds of data it's possible to generate through text mining practices.

As an example of a research project conducted by digital means, Matthew Jockers uses text mining to carry out what he calls "macroanalysis" on a corpus of several thousand nineteenth-century British novels using a range of different techniques.[6] To summarize (and more details below), Jockers is able to build arguments about literary style, theme, and influence by interpreting the results produced by computational methods. Working on a corpus of novels that no single author (or even sizable team of authors) could give fair treatment to using "conventional" research techniques, text and data mining allows Jockers to see inside of thousands of texts and find meaningful features using his years as a literary scholar as a guide.

Many tools can be used to accomplish these forms of analysis. See Bamboo DiRT for a quite comprehensive list of textual analysis tools (http://dirt.projectbamboo

.org/). For beginners, a web-based option such as Voyant Tools provides a good, easy to use introduction to many of the most widely used techniques that can be performed on digital texts (http://voyant-tools.org/). For most full-scale literary projects, however—especially those working with large corpora—a more tailored algorithm produced using customized scripts is often necessary. The programming language R (http://www.r-project.org/) and the Python Natural Language Tool Kit (NLTK; http://nltk.org/) library are examples of more full-bodied environments for processing and analyzing texts. In short, text-mining projects can be undertaken from a range of skill levels, and from varying degrees of comfort with coding and working at the command prompt. Text mining has become widespread enough that there is an appropriate tool for every kind of user.

LIBRARY CONNECTIONS

Librarians would do well to be interested in text mining for a range of reasons, the first of which is to support the latest forms of research being employed in humanities departments. Librarians have long worked to develop the subject knowledge that allows them to liaise with faculty members effectively, and to be keen selectors of new material for library acquisition following trends in current scholarship. A working familiarity with text-mining practice would extend that focus on domain expertise into directions becoming increasingly relevant to many humanists.

On a deeper level, though, text mining has the potential to draw researchers and librarians closer together in their scholarly and professional interests. First, data and text mining offer ways to open up content to new uses that would benefit the community served by the library generally. Librarians are tasked not simply with making resources *available*, but with making them *usable*. The use of digital texts increasingly involves computational and data-oriented methods of engagement. To improve the usability of digital collections, then, librarians have the opportunity to add value to text corpora by opening them up to these new forms of use, by considering text-mining approaches when selecting materials for purchase, and by making existing digital text collections as open to computational access as possible.

Further, humanities scholars and librarians alike are concerned with the value and implications of textual description, or markup. There is some shared theoretical ground here. The website of the Text Encoding Initiative (TEI), a consortium concerned with the representation of textual documents in digital form, remarks that "since 1994, the TEI Guidelines have been widely used by libraries, museums, publishers, and individual scholars to present texts for online research, teaching, and preservation."[7] Here in one succinct statement, digital humanities researchers and libraries are brought together by a shared concern with the organization and presentation of text. Both parties are interested in supporting the new forms of research that digital text helps engender. The structuring of text helps make text analysis projects more possible, by making text conform to the principles of structured data. In the context of her discussion about the commensurability of digital and traditional humanistic methods, Johanna Drucker states that "the tasks of creating metadata, doing markup, and making classification schemes or information architectures forced humanists to make explicit many assumptions often left implicit" in non-digital contexts.[8] What she's describing is precisely library work. Librarians have always been tasked with making interpretive judgments explicit, as a means of organizing information and allowing for access. Digital humanists are now doing the same. With this new common terrain, theoretical questions appear that could form the basis for shared research, or at least friendly commiseration: At what point does markup cross over from neutral description to interpretive judgment? In a world of information in which an infinite number of classificatory lenses might be applied, how do we justify the basis for some over others? Literary scholars and librarians are both concerned with how notions of categorization and classification change with time, and in how classificatory decisions themselves reflect the subjectivities of the individuals applying them. The digital humanities approach to text analysis seems poised to shorten the distance between interpretation and classification, between librarian and humanist.

Thus issues surrounding the analysis of digital text can also tighten the connections between librarians and other faculty researchers through shared scholarly interests. Yet the results of such research may also serve to benefit the library by enriching digital collections. Using existing knowledge of the contents of a given body of text allows librarians to perform targeted textual analysis. For instance, finding and annotating significant names or places can significantly enhance a user's experience of a digital collection. The University of Nebraska's Willa Cather Archive (http://cather.unl.edu/), for instance, greatly benefits from a robust attention to the embedded content of Cather's journals. A writer's private writings are often full of references to the people and places familiar to her, and of her time, but which may no longer be so familiar to modern readers. Finding and inserting appropriate links into the text of the archival materials for online display adds value for the reader by connecting unfamiliar names to descriptions, images, and the other locations in the archive where the same entity is mentioned.

Researchers are interested in the historical biography such markup highlights, and librarians are interested in the potential for collocating resources and improving user experience (though in practice the two sets of concerns are not so easily distinguished). Analyzing texts to uncover connections within the content improves usability and facilitates scholarly research.

Another distinct value that text mining holds for librarians can be found in the need to generate high-quality descriptive metadata. Creating metadata for large amounts of unknown or unstructured text may be cumbersome, or impossible, given limitations on time and expertise. As part of an archival project for the Center for Black Music Research, I used text mining to find appropriate keywords for use in a digital collection of oral history transcripts. Because the oral histories featured jazz musicians discussing aspects of their own personal biographies and musical upbringing, it was easy to note that musical genre could be a key factor in highlighting an important theme across the interview material. Comparing each interview text to a master list of over two hundred musical genres, and compiling lists of each genre mentioned in each interview, along with its frequency, allowed us to generate a network of musical genres across the set of interviews, reflecting the diverse backgrounds of these musicians (most of whom lived in or around London, but hailed from the Caribbean and West Africa, and thus invoked genres distinctly from those parts of the world such as reggae, soca, and highlife). Knowing which genre names appeared in which interviews—again, along with the frequencies of these terms—provided us with a means for mapping a framework of knowledge onto the interview texts by incorporating these excavated genre terms into metadata records. Analyzing the text using an algorithm to isolate mentions of genre produced a set of useful keywords for navigating the collection, while establishing a vocabulary that brought like musicians together, and revealed in a straightforward, potentially visual way the distances of influence between the entire group of musicians.

Text-mining procedures can also be used to gather specific named entities from within a text. These "named entities" might be persons, places, or organizations that could be discovered within large bodies of text through computational means. The occurrence or relative frequency of mentions for these names could then be used as access points for digital items or in cataloging records, or for building more interesting visual complements to digital collections, such as maps showing all the locations mentioned in a work of fiction.

Beyond finding specific names or other significant terms (such as musical genres) within a text, text mining gives librarians the chance to actually generate

91

descriptions of broader thematic content. While using specific words is one way to get at the content of text, describing the more general theme and scope of a text comes closer to capturing the "aboutness" of a work that librarians usually seek to describe using something like subject headings. Yet in moving from sets of words, which computers can gather and isolate, to satisfyingly comprehensive topical descriptions—often using words not actually found in the text—one must bridge a gap that as of now is really only possible to cross by means of human thought. The currently ascendant digital method of topic modeling, however, is one way of ever so slightly narrowing the gap between word and concept. Topic modeling offers an automated means of finding statistically significant word co-incidence: that is, topic modeling seeks to find which words tend to co-occur across a corpus of texts, and then to generate word frequency distributions of these co-occurring word sets. These frequency distributions are themselves what constitute a "topic" using this technique. Every word in a text from within that corpus can then be "explained" in terms of the presence of a given topic. Matthew Jockers uses topic modeling as part of his larger macroanalytic project on a set of nineteenth-century novels. Jockers worked from a corpus of several thousand texts, and directed the topic-modeling algorithm to generate five hundred "topics" from this corpus that then can be seen to be expressed to varying levels within each text.

For instance, a topic related to whaling and seafaring is particularly strong in *Moby-Dick* and might have a significant amount of explanatory power as far as predicting the words that appear in that book, but the same topic likely wouldn't appear at all in *Pride and Prejudice*.[9] Capturing these thematically inclined topics across the corpus allows Jockers to make claims about how theme, style, genre, and even author biography are connected: Do certain themes tend to occur more frequently in the work of female authors? What themes best characterize the picaresque novel compared to the bildungsroman?

Again, these topics are word-frequency distributions, not keyword-style terms or phrases. Yet these word-list topics can offer a sense of the range of thematic content contained within this corpus of fiction, and then about its individual works. For instance, a model employed by Jockers generated a topic with high frequencies for words such as *prisoner, murder, witness,* and *jury,* which a human reader might then render with a heading such as "Crime and Justice."[10] Thus the model returns sets of words that tend to point toward topical description as we usually think of it; that is, in a way that could help a librarian generate subject-style terms from lists of words without having read the original source texts. The algorithm cannot, at present, generate concept words from its word-frequency distributions, but it can help guide a human reader toward making an educated leap in that direction.

Text mining combined, particularly, with other librarian skills can yield valuable results. For instance, if a set of texts are known to cover twentieth-century painting, topic modeling can yield the specific words that are employed to describe this subject, as well as their varying relevance to each individual document within the collection. Therefore topic modeling can help discover points of both collocation and distinction between resources.

THE FUTURE OF TEXT MINING IN THE LIBRARY

Librarians who have become early adopters of text-analysis techniques are collaborating with faculty directly on projects that produce results of scholarly interest as well as enhance the library's digital collections. They are striving to make text mining more available to more users, including undergraduates. Publishers are increasingly responding to academic demand by making texts available for digital research: Libraries should do the same when it's in their power to do so. The new frontiers of the digital humanities allow librarians the chance to reconsider their notions of content and access. The lines between "data" and "information" are blurrier than ever, and access to either does not simply imply possession of a resource, but rather having within one's grasp the means of putting it to use in a range of data-driven and computational techniques.

Fitting skills such as text mining within the boundaries of librarianship, though, might need to involve both conceptual and administrative flexibility. Librarians pursuing digital humanities–oriented research may be accommodated within existing humanities librarianship frameworks, relating to their work to liaisonship, instruction, selection, and reference; or they may occupy other more nebulous positions. Each individual scenario generates its own unique benefits and difficulties. Institutions that are heavily invested in the digital humanities have created centers devoted to the promotion and incubation of new forms of digital scholarship, of which librarians may be a part. As Miriam Posner puts it in the opening sentences of her essay on administrative support for librarian digital humanities work, this "support might consist of a 'center,' a 'suite of services,' a librarian with a revised job title, or, murkiest of all, an 'initiative.' (A place, a thing, a person? Who knows?)"[11] It seems as though the digital humanities is an idea with enough momentum in the library to generate some institutional movement, though not always in clear directions. Digital humanities centers can focus creative work in one place with broad institutional support, but they can also become isolated individual units removed from other units, teams, committees, centers, organizations, departments, and individuals with whom they should be collaborating.

Or can this sort of isolation actually be productive, as a sort of insulation from politically motivated border disputes? Neil Fraistat, the director of the Maryland Institute for Technology in the Humanities (MITH), a DH center at the University of Maryland, points out that the "perceived tensions between 'research' and 'service' centers . . . create professional hierarchies that can inhibit the formation of potentially fruitful collaborations."[12] The division between research and service is a particular concern for libraries, where the service motive is often enunciated especially strongly. Bethany Nowviskie speaks of the virtues of allocating dedicated space and time for new forms of research in a sort of amorphous research zone known as a "skunkworks," here defined as a "small and nimble technical team, deliberately, and (yes) quite *unfairly* freed from much of the surrounding bureaucracy of the larger organization in which it locates itself."[13] This semi-independent unit provides an apt metaphor for the role text-mining and related skills play in the library. That is, it can be difficult to accommodate such digital methods in what we often call the "traditional" library (though it is worth rethinking and perhaps redefining this conventional conception), without stretching the definition of the library's role within the university, or operating at a slight remove from it.[14] Nowviskie sees the potential for "an organizational experiment in breaking away from shop-worn service relationships."[15] Text-mining skills seem to point away from these service relationships and toward more collaborative models of interaction with the library, but the indication is by no means absolute. The library might instead decide to use the service mission as its chief point of entry into the world of text-mining research, crafting a set of "text services" to be offered to interested collaborators and rendered as another way the library supports research in all its forms on campus.

The library, in coming years, while still remaining a bastion of print culture, will also become increasingly digital. Not only will more materials be online in digital form, but these digital materials will be accessible in more sophisticated ways that should reflect the input of librarians. Just reading text online will not account for the full breadth of the experience the digital text can engender. Using texts in novel ways will come to play a larger role in defining the experience. Texts will be available in raw or marked-up forms; users will be able to mine the full text of public domain or fully library-owned works, find connections between works that librarians have established, and build their own connections using tools that librarians have devised or implemented. The potential for increasing the usefulness of texts in these ways is vast. The movement from content that can be accessed, to content that can be used or transformed in creative ways, will continue forward, despite the threats imposed by current copyright law.

The legally ambiguous status of much of the digital text currently available online poses challenges to researchers. In the wake of the Google Books settlement of 2009, the idea of "non-consumptive" research has emerged as an escape clause.[16] Since computational methods such as text mining don't result in public or personal display of their source texts, these were considered to be "non-consumptive" and therefore exempt from certain copyright restrictions. The HathiTrust Research Center (www.hathitrust.org/htrc) is a large-scale attempt to expose a digital archive to advanced computational research, while ensuring that researchers stay within the boundaries of the "non-consumptive," never running algorithms that substantially recreate the works in the digital library for display or reading. Likewise, the Michigan State University Libraries (my own institution) are also hosting the set of Google-digitized public domain volumes and offering researchers an interface to access and download customized data sets of full text. The impulse of researchers to employ digital forms of research is well established, but the means of delivery is still under construction.

THE TEXT MINING HORIZON

Text mining will hold continued fascination for as long as it pushes new perspectives forward. In his manifesto for "algorithmic criticism," Stephen Ramsay argues against using text analysis and digital transformation exclusively as a means of applying "scientific" techniques to humanistic inquiries; he instead focuses on how the same techniques can be a source of rejuvenation and estrangement.[17] Text mining has the potential to return the text we know to us in a strange and altered form. The formalists' concept of *ostranenie*, in which the role of literature is to defamiliarize common language, fits as a clear literary precursor. Today's algorithmic critics and computational librarians are using text mining not only to deconstruct or categorize the texts on which they work, but to replenish them; to find new ways of seeing through experimental approaches. Ramsay's argument reflects the idea that these "new" techniques need not always be configured as separate from, or replacements for, traditional critical approaches in the humanities. Rather, as text mining becomes more familiar through repeated use (and possibly due to the embrace these methods have received by applications in commerce and advertising, of which more below), the techniques will become easier to integrate into the interpretive approaches we currently do not consider "new." However, text mining is not itself a form of criticism; it is the means of generating new critical forms through a distinct type of computational practice. Text mining is an always unfinished set of algorithms. Though some may achieve prominence and become established (topic modeling, for instance), the potential will always exist to build new approaches.

The same will hold true in the library. Text mining has the potential to define a set of practices that the librarian of the future will consider as standard components of her workflow, though these won't be competencies for all librarians to possess. The analogy to the recent debate about how "essential" coding is to librarians may make for a very close match: while there has been some push for librarians to become more skillful computer programmers, against some resistance, it seems sensible to think that even as the Venn diagram of librarianship and coding will increasingly show overlap, there will likely remain for quite some time, if not always, a majority of librarians for whom coding is harmlessly alien. Text-mining skills may be on the way to attaining the status of coding in general, that is, "weakly essential"—a skill that not all need to practice, but about which having a general familiarity is beneficial.[18]

While this chapter has focused on the connections between libraries and the digital humanities, the utility of text mining is far from contained within these contexts. The worlds of business, marketing and advertising have devoted resources to using text mining to "convert[ing] . . . user-generated content to market structures and competitive landscape insights."[19] In other words, the text voluntarily created by users (and contributed to social media platforms) amounts to a treasure trove of data ready to be mined to better understand consumer behavior. Companies will use the results of these mining projects to understand what consumers want, which forms of advertising are successful, and how to reach particular target populations. The business world's utilization of text mining and the movement of humanists toward embracing the potentialities of digital text are, after all, not so different in kind. Both reflect a response to a condition in the world: the staggering amount of text that we read, that we create, that besets us. In 2010, Google estimated that there were 129,864,880 books in the world.[20] UNESCO statistics indicate millions more are added to the total of published works every year, in an ever-increasing frenzy of publication.[21] Further, in our current age of big data, estimating just how much information there actually is in the world, or on the Internet, or even in Facebook's database alone, is a seemingly insurmountable task. Thinking up mind-blowing comparisons that will give us even some sense of the amounts of data our lives generate is its own cottage industry; even back in 2011, one could encounter a headline such as "Every Six Hours, the NSA Gathers as Much Data as Is Stored in the Entire Library of Congress."[22] The fact is, we are not able to "read" or otherwise process this data all on our own, in our own minds. So, what can we do with it? How can we generate any meaning at all from the massive stores of text and data that populate just our local corners of the digital universe? As long as we are faced with such mystifyingly large amounts of textual information, we will seek strategies for dealing with it, even if that strategy is to ignore it. Yet the continual development of techniques for reckoning with so much text signifies that we will also carry on, as ever, doing what we can to build truer-seeming structures of meaning from the language that surrounds us, no matter what form that language takes.

NOTES

1. Ted Underwood, "On Not Trusting People Who Promise 'To Use Their Powers for Good,'" *The Stone and the Shell* (blog), June 11, 2013, http://tedunderwood .com/2013/06/11/on-not-trusting-people-who-promise-to-use-their-powers-for -good/.

2. Emile Durkheim, *Suicide: A Study in* Sociology, trans. John A. Spaulding and George Simpson (New York: The Free Press, 1951).

3. Franco Moretti, "Conjectures on World Literature," *New Left Review* (2000), 54–68.

4. Jon Orwant, "Ngram Viewer 2.0," *Google Research Blog*, October 18, 2012, http:// googleresearch.blogspot.com/2012/10/ngram-viewer-20.html.

5. David Greetham, "The Resistance to the Digital Humanities," in *Debates in the Digital Humanities*, ed. Matthew K. Gold (Minneapolis: University of Minnesota Press, 2012), 439.

6. Matthew Jockers, *Macroanalysis: Digital Methods and Literary History* (Urbana: University of Illinois Press, 2013).

7. Text Incoding Initiative (website), accessed March 15, 2014, www.tei-c.org/ index.xml.

8. Johanna Drucker, "Humanistic Theory and Digital Scholarship," in *Debates in the Digital Humanities*, ed. Matthew K. Gold (Minneapolis: University of Minnesota Press, 2012), 85.

9. Jockers, *Macroanalysis*, 130.

10. Matthew Jockers, "'Secret' Recipe for Topic Modeling Themes," *Matthew L. Jockers* (blog), April 12, 2013, www.matthewjockers.net/2013/04/12/secret-recipe-for-topic -modeling-themes/.

11. Miriam Posner, "No Half Measures: Overcoming Common Challenges to Doing Digital Humanities in the Library," UCLA, accessed August 18, 2013, doi:10.1080/01 930826.2013.756694.

12. Neil Fraistat, "The Function of Digital Humanities Centers at the Present Time," in *Debates in the Digital Humanities*, ed. Matthew K. Gold (Minneapolis: University of Minnesota Press, 2012), 282.

13. Bethany Nowviskie, "Skunks in the Library: A Path to Production for Scholarly R&D," *Journal of Library Administration* 53, no. 1 (2012): 56.

14. Trevor Muñoz, "In Service? A Further Provocation on Digital Humanities Research in Libraries," *dh+lib* (blog), June 19, 2013, http://acrl.ala.org/dh/2013/06/19/in-service -a-further-provocation-on-digital-humanities-research-in-libraries/.

15. Nowviskie, "Skunks in the Library," 59.

16. John Unsworth, "Computational Work with Very Large Text Collections," *Journal of the Text Encoding Initiative* 1 (2011), accessed September 23, 2013, doi:10.4000/ jtei.215.

17. Stephen Ramsay, *Reading Machines: Toward an Algorithmic Criticism*. Urbana: University of Illinois Press, 2011.

18. Lane Wilkinson, "Is Coding an Essential Library Skill?" *Sense and Reference* (blog), March 8, 2013, http://senseandreference.wordpress.com/2013/03/08/is-coding-an -essential-library-skill/.

19. Oded Netzer et al. "Mine Your Own Business: Market-Structure Surveillance through Text Mining," *Marketing Science* 31.3 (2012): 521, accessed August 18, 2013, doi:10.1287/mksc.1120.0713.

20. Leonid Taycher, "You Can Count the Number of Books in the World on 25,972,976 hands," *Google Official Blog* (blog), August 5, 2010, http://googleblog.blogspot.com/ 2010/08/you-can-count-number-of-books-in-world.html.

21. "Books Published in the World—Sources and Methods," Worldometers, accessed August 18, 2013, www.worldometers.info/books/.

22. Dan Nosowitz, "Every Six Hours, the NSA Gathers as Much Data as Is Stored in the Entire Library of Congress," *Popular Science*, May 10, 2011, www.popsci.com/ technology/article/2011-05/every-six-hours-nsa-gathers-much-data-stored-entire -library-congress.

FOR FURTHER READING

A Companion to Digital Humanities. Blackwell Companions to Literature and Culture 26. Malden, Mass.: Blackwell Publishing, 2004. http://ezproxy.msu.edu:2047/

login?url=http://www.blackwellreference.com/subscriber/book?id=g9781405103213
9781405103213.

Blei, David M. "Topic Modeling and Digital Humanities." *Journal of Digital Humanities* (April 8, 2013). http://journalofdigitalhumanities.org/2-1/topic-modeling-and-digital-humanities-by-david-m-blei/.

Brett, Megan R. "Topic Modeling: A Basic Introduction." *Journal of Digital Humanities* (April 8, 2013). http://journalofdigitalhumanities.org/2-1/topic-modeling-a-basic-introduction-by-megan-r-brett/.

Burton, Matt. "The Joy of Topic Modeling," n.d., http://mcburton.net/blog/joy-of-tm/.

Darnton, Robert. "5 Myths About the 'Information Age.'" *The Chronicle of Higher Education*, April 17, 2011. http://chronicle.com/article/5-Myths-About-the-Information/127105/.

Enis, Matt. "Cracking the Code: Librarians Acquiring Essential Coding Skills." *The Digital Shift*. Accessed August 19, 2013. http://www.thedigitalshift.com/2013/03/software/cracking-the-code/.

Johnston, Leslie. "How Many Libraries of Congress Does It Take?" *The Signal: Digital Preservation* (blog). March 23, 2012. http://blogs.loc.gov/digitalpreservation/2012/03/how-many-libraries-of-congress-does-it-take/.

Liu, Alan. "The Meaning of the Digital Humanities." *PMLA* 128.2 (2013).

Meeks, Elijah, and Scott B. Weingart. "The Digital Humanities Contribution to Topic Modeling." *Journal of Digital Humanities* (April 8, 2013). http://journalofdigitalhumanities.org/2-1/dh-contribution-to-topic-modeling/.

Practical Text Mining and Statistical Analysis for Non-structured Text Data Applications. 1st ed. Waltham, MA: Academic Press, 2012. http://ezproxy.msu.edu:2047/login?url=http://www.sciencedirect.com/science/book/9780123869791.

Schmidt, Desmond. "The Role of Markup in the Digital Humanities." *Historical Social Research* 37, no. 3 (2012): 125–146.

Underwood, Ted. "Where to Start with Text Mining." *The S*. Accessed August 19, 2013. http://tedunderwood.com/2012/08/14/where-to-start-with-text-mining/.

———. "Wordcounts Are Amazing." *The Stone and the Shell*. Accessed June 24, 2013. http://tedunderwood.com/2013/02/20/wordcounts-are-amazing/.

Zimmer, Ben. "A New Chapter for Google Ngrams." *Language Log*. Accessed August 19, 2013. http://languagelog.ldc.upenn.edu/nll/?p=4258.

Bigger, Better, Together
Building the Digital Library of the Future

Jeremy York

Whether we are sitting down to write a term paper, researching our family history, gathering information about an illness, or simply looking for a good book or movie to occupy our time, we are united by common desires in seeking information: we want it here, we want it free, we want it now. In the last several decades, there have been numerous developments that have served both to speed and to frustrate the fulfillment of these desires—from the development of computers and the Internet to movements for free and open software on one hand, to the monetization of digital access, aggressive licensing, and digital rights management on the other.

The cultural heritage community has not been removed from these developments and struggles. In recent years we have seen a redevelopment and retooling of cultural heritage institutions as they seek to fulfill their traditional missions to preserve and provide access to our collected heritage and knowledge. A major development in this remaking process has been the formation of large-scale collaborative initiatives—among libraries in particular, but among archives, museums, and other cultural heritage institutions as well. Some of the initiatives seek to aggregate large amounts of materials digitized from their institutional collections either for purposes of preservation or access or for both. Europeana, HathiTrust, and the Digital Public Library of America are some of the most prominent examples, and there are others as well. This chapter examines the work of large-scale digital initiatives today and explores the directions they might take over the next several years. Three key elements will guide the discussion: the underlying data the various initiatives seek to preserve and make accessible; the types of collaboration involved; and the services they make available to end users.

THE DATA

I remember when I was young being captivated by the "Computer" in *Star Trek: The Next Generation*—how Captain Jean-Luc Picard could ask questions with equal ease about star maps and planetary systems, or passages of Shakespeare and literature from his distant past. What would it be like, I wondered, to have the resources of Computer at my disposal—and the capabilities of the character Data to read, digest, analyze, and understand galaxies' worth of information in a matter of microseconds? "Computer, give me the ten most authoritative analyses of Zora Neale Hurston's *Their Eyes Were Watching God*." "Computer. Give me everything you have on Teddy Roosevelt and the Spanish-American War." I would have aced my English and history exams (not so sure what would have happened with algebra).

Today I wonder what it would be like if we all had this kind of access? What if any of us could enter the Starship Enterprise's holodeck and in a matter of moments be walking through computer-generated versions of nineteenth-century New York, ancient Rome, or any place and time that we had sufficient data to recreate? What would our education be like, our entertainment and jobs, our political and social systems? Information is freedom and power. Access to information is transformative.

Information is also data. And data is where the rubber hits the road.

The data of our lives was once kept in our memories, or communicated in real time through sound waves from one of us to the other. Through time it has been inscribed on cave walls, clay tablets, and plants. It has been written and printed in books, on magnetic tape, and via other media. And now it is in digits. For the vast majority of human history, data from the world around us has been something that could be processed by human senses and the human brain. We were the primary processors, translating data into meaningful information. In digital form, for most of us (realizing some of us may read in hexadecimal), the data must be preprocessed and translated from binary representations in order to be made manifest in a form we can readily use.

There are great benefits to this arrangement, including the small size of digital data in comparison with analog, the ease of transmission, and the scope and sophistication of tools (from web browsers to Adobe products to 3-D design labs) that can be used to render the information to a broad variety of audiences. These strengths can also be weaknesses, however, as we know—particularly with regard to issues of authenticity, reliability, and preservation. The media we use for digital information are often fragile, easily subject to damage and decay, as well as malleable, subject to accidental change or intentional tampering. Securing the data, then, is a first priority and prerequisite to any kind of reliable or long-term use.

Significant progress has been made, beginning in the 1990s, on questions related to the preservation of digital materials, resulting in robust guidelines for creating and maintaining trustworthy repositories for digital data. As of this writing, four repositories in North American have been certified as "Trustworthy Digital Repositories" by the Center for Research Libraries (CRL), a body that has taken on the work of certification on behalf of its extensive community. These repositories are Portico, HathiTrust, Chronopolis, and Scholars Portal. Each of these repositories has a different focus and model of services: Portico preserves licensed e-book and e-journal content that it may make available separately from licensors in cases of designated "trigger events"; HathiTrust preserves and provides access to book and journal content digitized from partnering libraries; Chronopolis provides preservation services for a broad variety of data; Scholars Portal offers a wide range of content but has been certified in particular for its ability to manage electronic journal content. Even with their different foci and service models, these repositories share underlying missions to preserve digital content for their communities, and their formal certification contributes to their legitimacy and importance.

Of course, there are many more preservation efforts in existence than the ones that have been certified, and there are more frameworks in use to evaluate repositories than the framework used by the Center for Research Libraries. A significant number of academic, research, or governmental institutions in North America, Europe, Asia, and Australia have their own digital preservation programs, and a number of shared preservation initiatives—such as LOCKSS, CLOCKSS, MetaArchive, and the emergent Digital Preservation Network (DPN)—have gained increasing support and importance in recent years. Meanwhile, efforts such as the International Internet Preservation Consortium (comprising primarily national libraries from around the world, but also including nonprofit organizations such as the Internet Archive, Internet Memory Foundation, and National Film Board of Canada), are tackling issues around the preservation of the World Wide Web.

In the next several years, I believe we will see expanded collaboration among publishers, nonprofit organizations, and cultural heritage institutions to increase the amount of "secured" data that will flow, or at least have the possibility to flow, into the Computer of the future. There are a number of areas of concern, however, that are not necessarily covered by current initiatives, where I believe there will be progress in the near term, but where progress will be more slow. These concerns relate to the range of the participants involved in digital preservation initiatives and the scope of the data that is preserved.

In particular, while an increasing number of publishers and major academic institutions are securing more and more of their collections, there remain a large number of colleges and universities, archives, historical societies, public libraries, museums, and individuals with collections of importance that either are not on the map to digitize, or are digitized but with no plan for preservation. Furthermore, many institutions are only beginning to address the challenges of preserving legacy audio and video collections that are in grave danger of being lost due to obsolescence or decay. Initiatives to preserve new forms of digital production—including art, multimedia publications, games, and others—are also still building capacity. Some of the major challenges preservation initiatives will face in the next couple of years are to bring more organizations, institutions, corporations, and individuals into the scope of collaborative projects, and to develop strategies to identify and retain the materials, among all of those created, that are valuable to preserve over the long term.

COLLABORATION

For all of its processing power, the Computer in *Star Trek* would certainly not have been what it was without the vast database of information behind it, and the database was surely only as good as the information compiled from all its contributors. There are two main factors driving contributions to, and collaborations in, preservation and access initiatives for cultural heritage institutions today. The first is a deep commitment to the traditional roles our institutions have had as stewards and disseminators of our collected knowledge; if we do not this, there is no one with the knowledge, skill, and enduring interest (at least, in the long run) who will. While corporations and for-profit entities are critical partners, their interests do not necessarily align with interests of the scholarly and educational communities. At the same time, academic and cultural heritage institutions are not without their own bottom lines. If libraries at universities, for instance, do not meet the needs of their students, faculty, and staff, they run the risk of losing administrative support and being marginalized as information sources for their constituencies. The same could be said of any public library, historical society, museum, or other similar institution. The second major factor, then, is the knowledge that we will never be as comprehensive as we would like and will never be as comprehensive and financially feasible as we must be if we do not combine our efforts and collaborate effectively in areas where collaboration is a possibility. Realizing the value of our collections and services in aggregate is the Web 2.0 of digital initiatives.

HathiTrust is an exemplar of a new kind of collaboration that libraries are seeking in order to prepare themselves not just to be relevant, but to be leaders and innovators in the next century. HathiTrust is a broad collaboration of academic and research institutions that are pooling efforts to preserve and provide access to "the record of human knowledge."[1] The partnership launched a large-scale digital repository in 2008, which currently contains close to 11 million volumes digitized from their library collections. Nearly 3.5 million of these are in the public domain and available on the Web.

There are a number of aspects that make collaboration in HathiTrust different from collaborations in the past. The first is the depth of collaboration. Rather than being a common software package that institutions have implemented separately to preserve and provide access to their collections, or a place where institutions are *also* putting their digitized materials to provide access to them, HathiTrust is a deep sharing of content where institutions' preservation copies are being placed in a repository that is owned and managed collaboratively by the partner institutions. It is a shared collection on a scale that we have never before seen. The partners believe that this kind of sharing is the best way to maximize the cost efficiency and impact of services offered for the deposited materials. They are not building and operating multiple systems individually; they are building one system, with adequately distributed components, together.

The second difference in HathiTrust is in the scope of the collaboration. The scope of HathiTrust's mission and goals extends to helping institutions address the long-term costs associated with the storage and management of print materials, as well as to developing new models of scholarly publishing. By sharing in the management of a collective collection of digital materials, libraries have the possibility of gaining a greater understanding of correspondences between all their collections, whether in analog form or digital. Through shared goals and shared governance, libraries have the capacity to coordinate decisions about the materials that are accessioned, retained, or deaccessioned from the shared collection and from their local collections. Libraries are able to make decisions—informed by collective holdings—about how best to allocate time and resources to most effectively meet the needs of their communities.

With regard to publishing, the base of financial and organizational stability that is achieved through broad participation in HathiTrust allows for exploration of new possibilities and new models. In particular, HathiTrust is pursuing an initiative to allow publishing of open access materials directly into the repository, thus combining processes involved in publication and archiving, and opening a new channel for libraries and publishers with common interests to work together toward common ends.

HathiTrust is a prime example of twenty-first-century library collaboration, but it is by no means the only example. Europeana, the Digital Public Library of America (DPLA), the Digital Preservation Network (DPN), and other repository efforts mentioned above are premised on the value that can be gained from leveraging resources in aggregate. The DPLA seeks to aggregate and provide access to publicly available materials of all kinds through a platform that allows sharing and integration in the widest possible number of contexts and applications. The DPLA is an access layer that leverages both individual preservation infrastructures at institutions it aggregates from, and collective preservation infrastructures, such as HathiTrust, in order to provide reliable access. The DPN, for its part, is a collaboration seeking to build a preservation safety net that underlies collaborative repositories in order to ensure durable access to the scholarly record. We are seeing today an increase in collaboration among libraries and other cultural heritage institutions across shared areas of interest (e.g., preservation, access, or publishing). We are also seeing, in aggregate, the emergence of a new library ecosystem. In this ecosystem, different collaborations are taking complementary roles and functions, becoming systems of collaborations, united by common desires to better serve local and collective user communities more effectively and at lower cost.

I believe that broadening collaboration, leveraging resources in aggregate, and developing collaborations with complementary roles and responsibilities are trends that will continue in the next couple of years. Some of the issues I believe are important to continued positive development in these areas are:

1. Models of governance that are adequately inclusive and representative of members, and at the same time nimble and efficient. There are particular issues in this arena regarding collaborations across governmental boundaries and legal regimes.

2. Continued alignment of the goals of collaborative enterprises with the goals of their participating members.

3. "Sourcing and scaling" of collaborative work. Sourcing and scaling are concepts that Lorcan Dempsey has written about; they involve identifying appropriate levels at which support for initiatives should be "sourced" and appropriate scales for collaboration to occur.[2] We know that collaboration is not appropriate for all activities; we know that the same level of collaboration is not effective for all undertakings. One of our greatest challenges going forward will be finding ways to source and scale initiatives in order to achieve optimum balances in efficiency, impact, and value.

SERVICES TO USERS

It is hard to imagine a service that could be better than one where it is possible to ask aloud any question you would like and immediately receive an answer. Right? "Computer, calculate the average rates of climate change over the last one hundred thousand, ten thousand, thousand, and hundred years, and model the effect of those changes over the next hundred years based on expected human social and political responses." I would say: not necessarily. For sure, we want to support full-text search across our collections where possible. For sure, we want users to be able to find our collections where relevant, no matter where they are searching. For sure, we want the most usable systems possible, overcoming all the attendant contradictions and challenges our user experience teams encounter every day. It is worth considering for a moment, however, where our current systems are taking us, and where we would like to be.

Although we have common desires in seeking information, we can have vastly differing skill sets, needs, and tolerances when it comes to the search process and using the information we find. Some of us seek information by querying resources directly through keyword searches or browsing tools. Some prefer to search via social networks or by examining citations in relevant books and articles. Sometimes we appreciate people or websites that remember our preferences or what we searched for the last time; sometimes we do not.

Below are some of the trends we are seeing today in user services (with *user* defined broadly as those who benefit from accessing the resource). These point the way to what we can expect to see more of in the future.

Making data available. One of the major trends taking place in digital repositories and digital resources in general today is a strong drive to provide access to underlying data: through linked data, APIs, data feeds—any ways that data can be made available for processing, recombination, and reuse. The availability of data facilitates its gathering and reuse by researchers. It is also a prerequisite for interoperability among administrative systems, and allows administrators to customize interfaces for their user communities, to test new functionality, and to build customized user services. APIs are key service features highlighted by HathiTrust, the DPLA, and Europeana.

Use and understand. A second major trend is a call from multiple sources for a shift from what Eric Lease Morgan has called "find and get" services, where the user puts information in a search box and selects from results, to "use and understand" services, where users are able to go beyond retrieving results to "doing" things with those results.[3] Some examples Morgan gives are the abilities to analyze, annotate, cite, compare and contrast, count and tabulate, discuss, evaluate, graph and visualize, and summarize discovered information. Morgan discusses how using text mining and natural-language processing in back-end processing can surface new information such as how long a book is (by word count rather than page), its reading difficulty, what concepts are present, the proximity of a particular word to other words, the location of a particular word within a text, and much more. Many types of analyses that have become more popular in recent years (e.g., word clouds, topic modeling, and network analyses) are based on these kinds of semantic processing. Ultimately, such processing and added functionality rely on the availability of underlying data, which enables researchers, application builders, and others to answer questions and meet their own needs, or the needs of their constituencies, through access to raw data.

Personalization and recommendation. Two other trends that are active today are an increase in personalization and in recommendation services. More and more in library and other information resources, we have the ability to customize dashboards, save personal collections, and set resource preferences. Interfaces and services respond to the devices we use, the locations we are accessing from, the information we last accessed, and our account privileges. Systems may also suggest alternate resources based on our search terms, browsing history, or resources others have viewed. Services are being designed not only to allow us to find information and do interesting things with it, but also to respond to our behaviors and preferences—and sometimes even our physical movements as well.

What do these trends mean for collaborations between large academic and cultural heritage institutions, and for the digital library of the future?

- There will certainly be a greater availability of data, including new data created or derived from the primary data.
- We will certainly provide more tools and opportunities for users to do interesting things with data.
- We will almost certainly be gathering and using more information about our users via the provision of services.

All of these have important implications, but the last in particular is worth considering with some care as we go forward. Part of what is driving our collaborations today, and innovations in services, is the knowledge that we, as stewards of our cultural heritage, must continue to change and adapt to the new information environment in order to be true to our missions, convictions, and values, and, at a minimum, to continue to be relevant in a culture that seeks information free, here, and now. As corporations innovate their consumer services, users approach libraries and other institutions with expectations that impact the services we offer. A single search box is a great example; streamlined interface designs and the use of analytics to determine how our websites are used and how they can be configured to best meet the needs of our users are others.

There are some issues I believe it is crucial to keep in mind as we move forward in the services we offer. The first is the particular constituencies and particular needs we are trying to meet. Education today is ever more commoditized, but it is important for us to pay attention to the actual trends and innovations happening in educational services. Some of these are:

- trends in approaches to learning that are more entrepreneurial, playful, interdisciplinary, and collaborative
- trends toward "active classrooms" and greater involvement of students in designing the learning experience
- trends toward increased peer critique

We should not only concern ourselves with offering improved personalization services, but with how our services can support greater collaboration, greater

109

entrepreneurship, greater empowerment of students in creating, both individually and collectively, their own learning experiences. Because of our deep experience and ties to the educational and scholarly communities, these areas may be ones in which we as libraries and cultural heritage institutions are well placed to innovate.

Another crucial issue is the traditional value that cultural heritage institutions place on maintaining and protecting the privacy of our patrons. The relationship of trust that we have as a community with our users has been built over literally centuries of time. There are numerous threats to this relationship today, including from governmental forces completely removed from issues related to the enhancement of user services. As we go forward, I believe our institutions must ensure the strength of this relationship, through transparency about our data collection practices, through opt-in and opt-out strategies, through any means at our disposal. The trust that we have with our users is one of the greatest values we bring to the marketplace of information, and is another area in which, in the twenty-first century, we are well placed to be the innovators.

PREPARING FOR SUCCESS

I'm not sure if anyone has ever said that reputation is the enemy of collaboration, but the relationship between these elements is something that cultural heritage institutions should consider carefully. For centuries our institutions have built their reputations on how much data they hold. They have amassed information, and have grown in prestige from the fact that that information could be made available only to a select few to digest and impart to others. The winds of sharing are changing, however. From open-source software to open-access licenses, from open educational resources to massive open online courses, more and more prestige is being ascribed to institutions that share their resources and expertise, and collaborate with others. Over the next several years I think the boundaries of sharing and reputation will be tested. If we get it right—if our institutions and collaborations are able to source and scale appropriately so that we do in fact maximize our value and impact—it is a very real possibility that a significant portion of our data sharing services will become part of the invisible infrastructure that underlies our collective web of knowledge. If all our data is made available (as much as it can be, bounded by respect for copyright law and concerns about user privacy), the exact source of the information may become less important to researchers and scholars than the fact that the information is available at all, and that it is trustworthy. If a researcher knows that materials are made available via HathiTrust, for instance, or provided through the DPLA, the particular institution that contributed the material may fade into the background. To the external observer, the collaborations become great, and individual institution may be accorded status because of their participation in the collaborations, rather than because they have achieved greatness on their own.

There is a fear in this for libraries and other cultural heritage institutions; a fear that a lack of acknowledgement and recognition, if it were to occur, would lead to less funding and less capability to make information available and offer important services. I believe that the more we pool our resources and learn to work together, the stronger we will be. But we must get the balances of contributed effort and recognition correct. The progress we make in the next few years toward better services and more efficient operations will depend less on what we are technically capable of and more on the perceived value of our collective activities to ourselves and to those who fund our institutions and programs. As measures of external prestige shift from holding data to sharing data, and from sharing data to packaging data and offering personalized services in the future, we must be sure within our collaborations that appropriate means of attribution and recognition continue to exist for all activities. This is the job of the governance we choose to take us forward: to help us see the value we can achieve by acting collectively, and to ensure that when others see the power of our results, they know who was responsible for getting us there.

SOME FINAL WORDS ABOUT TRUST AND THE *STAR TREK* COMPUTER OF THE FUTURE

We should always be suspicious of information. Just as we cannot always trust our senses and perceptions, we cannot always trust the data we encounter to be accurate or the algorithms and processes running across the data to be correct or functioning properly. We are living our lives somewhat in translation in the information age, often having multiple layers of technology between us and other people; between us and the answers we seek. Our Computer of the future, if it is to serve the needs of humankind—if it is to help build a more just, free, and equal society—must be built on trust. Those of us with responsibility for collecting, preserving, and sharing our collected knowledge and creativity must continue in the best traditions of our field. We must secure the data. We must work to ensure that the data is lawfully accessible for purposes of education and governance, and as a matter of public policy. We must be flexible, entrepreneurial, and innovative. We must keep our purpose and the needs of our communities at the forefront of our minds. And we must work together.

NOTES

1. "Mission and Goals," accessed August 13, 2013, HathiTrust, www.hathitrust.org/mission_goals.

2. Lorcan Dempsey, "Sourcing and Scaling," *Lorcan Dempsey's Weblog*, February 21, 2010, http://orweblog.oclc.org/archives/002058.html.

3. Eric Lease Morgan, "Use & Understand: A DPLA beta-sprint proposal," Infomotions, September 1, 2011, http://infomotions.com/blog/2011/09/dpla/.

The Case for Open Hardware in Libraries

Jason Griffey

Over the last couple of years, a slow transformation has taken place within libraries. It's happening in small ways in many places, but the drive toward understanding the library as a center for creation of things—as opposed to a center for preservation and consumption of information—seems to have struck a chord. There are a number of ways this has happened and is happening, from the media centers that you can find in many libraries where patrons are creating audio and video content, to the movement of the moment, makerspaces in libraries.[1] From the media center to the makerspace, patrons are creating their own texts, music, video, and now objects via 3-D printers and CNC (computer numerical control) routers at libraries. The modern library is not for consumption only (not that it ever has been), but for creation and distribution of works.

But this move toward making is interesting in several ways. The rise of media creation came, at least partially, from the rise of libraries using the tools involved in their own operations, much in the same way that public computers were rolled out to patrons in libraries after they had already become commonplace in the backroom operations of libraries. Libraries tend to "dogfood" their new technology—using it internally, or "eating your own dog food"—before rolling it out to the public, often without realizing that they are even in the process of doing so. Scanners were used in interlibrary loan and reserves long before they were provided to the public, and other technologies were well understood in the processes and procedures of the library before they had a public face.

Contrary to this model, the rise of the makerspace in the library seems to be driven by the desire to give the technology to the public, and not by a recognized need for the various technologies to improve the processes and procedures of the library itself. In this chapter I outline a rationale for just this idea: That moving into the next ten years of library operations, it will become increasingly important for libraries to embrace the variety of maker technologies in order to extend their services and assessment of services. I believe that having a makerspace/creation space is ultimately going to be more important for the library than it will for the patrons.

Finer minds than mine have argued that we are heading toward a technological era that will give rise to the post-mass-manufacturing production of goods. Increasingly inexpensive general-purpose computing hardware platforms such as the Raspberry Pi and Arduino provide the base for customizable hardware creation. Features such as 3-D printing, laser cutting, and CNC routers allow for the creation of physical objects, enclosures, and containers. When you combine these with the increasingly rich open-source/libre software collections driven by sites such as GitHub, you have the recipe for bespoke hardware, something that was out of reach for everyone except the very rich until now.

You've always had hardware hackers building away, famously, in their garages. Indeed, this very instinct gave rise to the personal computer revolution as we know it through people such as Steve Wozniak, Bill Gates, and the early homebrew computer clubs. But never has hardware been as easy to build from a recipe. It is very possible these days, if you have the infrastructure in place or a makerspace to visit, for you to read about a piece of hardware and build it yourself simply by following instructions: print this, download this program, copy to your board via USB, slide tab A into slot B, and you have your very own RFID reader, or gate counter, or video capture box. Libraries are currently beholden to vendors for a great deal of hardware, but this hardware is now within the realm of being something we could build ourselves.

But why should libraries bother? Moving to building our own hardware takes the same shift in understanding and economics that moving to open source software has taken in many libraries. Libraries can choose to place their cash into staff instead of into support contracts. Doing so gives libraries flexibility that they don't have with vendor-driven hardware, because it gives libraries the ability (again, just like with software) to make changes that benefit a particular situation and need. It also provides the ability to improve the hardware and software at the library's own pace—anyone who has dealt with any vendor has run into a situation where the speed with which you want change doesn't match the speed with which the vendor can make it change.

While these are sufficient reasons to pursue our own hardware, they aren't necessarily the most important. I believe that there are emergent reasons related to the increasingly digital nature of our work.

It isn't a secret that library services everywhere are moving increasingly digital. Even with the difficulties and challenges of e-books and other electronic content issues (licensing, DRM, etc.) taken into account. In many cases, digital means distant, and we are removing a lot of the need for patrons to come physically to our locations. My place of work is an academic library, and I assure you that most students do their research remotely, accessing library-provided databases from the comfort of their dorm or apartment. We attempt to catch as many students as possible during their required English classes to provide some library instruction/information literacy classes, and offer a bevy of other instructional opportunities to students, faculty, and staff.

The trend for most libraries, long term, is fewer in-person interactions and lower circulation of physical objects, at least as compared to the previous couple of decades. Meanwhile, we see a rise in digital delivery of content. Library circulation numbers are often buoyed by DVD checkouts, while Netflix and other streaming-video choices grow as a way of consuming video, preparing to bring circulation numbers down.

And yet when ACRL publishes summary statistics about libraries' performance, digital delivery of content is still listed in the "supplementary" section. Libraries are still measured against one another by physical collection size and circulation numbers, things that are increasingly unimportant in the actual delivery of our product to our patrons. How should we react to this?

I maintain that libraries would be far better off with new measurements of usage. The rise of custom hardware is potentially one answer for how we gain these measurements.

HARDWARE

One of the advantages of the meteoric uptake of mobile phones is that the cost of the sensors they use (microphones, cameras, accelerometers, GPS, light sensors, compasses, and much more) has been driven down to nothing. This has allowed the manufacturers of other devices to incorporate sensors where just five to seven years ago it would have been far too expensive. That, combined with the momentum of Moore's law, means that we now have the ability to manufacture—or more important, make for ourselves—electronics that can report things about the world in new ways.

Hardware projects such as Node (www.variabletech.com) and Twine (http://supermechanical.com/) show us that it's possible to build inexpensive sensor-driven hardware that is networked and capable of communicating with other systems—exactly the right sort of thing to have around if you are looking to find new things to measure in your library. Imagine the very near future, when it will be possible to measure not only how many people come into your library, but what books your patrons are looking at on the shelves and not checking out. Imagine knowing every time someone went into an aisle and moved a book. How rich a dataset could a library create about browsing habits, patron choices, and selection behaviors, and what could that do to our space planning, our acquisitions, and our programming planning if we had that kind of information?

While the growth of projects and products using open hardware is explosive, the actual hardware being used has standardized pretty heavily around just a couple of platforms. The two largest platforms for hardware at this point are Arduino and Raspberry Pi, with a long tail of other hardware for specialized uses available. If you understand these two, there really is very little limit to the sorts of things you can build. Combine these hardware building blocks with a 3-D printer, and you've got a completely packaged hardware solution, complete with case and mounting solution.

Arduino is the name of a type of open hardware, a particular type of board that has a wide variety of instantiations (Uno, Mega, Lilypad, Mini, Duemilanove, Esplora, and Due are just a few of the more popular models). It is a microcontroller, an integrated circuit that has a processor and memory, but most important, a series of input and output controllers. It's programmable via a very simple IDE (integrated development environment) that uses C and C++, but includes a software library called Wiring that makes many operations much simpler than writing raw C code.

Arduino has become the most popular style of microcontroller for small-electronics work because of its versatility and low price. While they vary in price greatly, you can find Arduinos for between $15 and $30, and once a program has been developed for an Arduino microprocessor, altering it and replicating it from board to board is very straightforward. This makes the development of a program that solves a specific problem replicable across libraries, in the same way that open-source software allows many libraries to benefit from the efforts of a few. You don't have to write the program for the Arduino; you just have to know where to get it and how to load it.

So what sort of things can you do with an Arduino? The simplest way to think about it is as an action and reaction machine. Anytime something happens, and then you want something else to happen, the Arduino can do that for you. Someone walks through your door, and you want to count it? Hook an Arduino up to a sensor and tell it to count whenever someone trips that sensor. When someone puts a book in your book return, do you want a robot to wave at them? You could do that as well. Arduinos are used for all sorts of robotic efforts, from Furby-like interactive robots to autonomous flying drones.

We will return to projects that libraries might want to implement using Arduino microprocessors in a bit. Let's take a look at Arduino's relative in open source hardware, Raspberry Pi.

The Raspberry Pi microprocessor is slightly different in design and use than an Arduino. It is also an open platform, but the Raspberry Pi is a full computer, with processor, RAM, and USB ports; an HDMI port for video out; an audio port; and an SD card port that used for the "hard drive" of the device. The Raspberry Pi also has an Ethernet port built in, to make hardwired networking straightforward. It will run a variety of operating systems, but most users settle on some form of Linux.

The Raspberry Pi, even though it is a fully-functional computer, costs $35–50 at retail in the United States. This low cost makes it ideal to implement things that require a bit more logic than simple input/output like an Arduino. Since the Raspberry Pi is just another Linux computer, it can do most of the same things that other Linux-based computers can do, albeit on a smaller scale or with a lower load. It can act as a server for any number of efforts, including as a web server. Many labs are using the Raspberry Pi as a development platform for individuals who are learning to code. Rather than having a single server that everyone shares, a lab can afford to allow each user to have their own personal server based on the Raspberry Pi to test everything from web apps to database management.

As a stand-alone computer, the Raspberry Pi is even suitable for low-power kiosk use. It will run a modern web browser and connect to an HDMI monitor, which means that for many library users, it may easily take care of their computing needs. It works very well as a front-end client for any number of display needs, and is one of the very cheapest options to get computer-driven visual content onto a screen.

Both platforms are popular enough that entire ecosystems of products revolve around them now. There is a thriving business in Arduino expansion boards, called

Shields, that give it additional capabilities. These include data-logging Shields that will write data collected out to SD cards or other memory, Shields that have sensors or LEDs built in that can react to stimuli, or Shields that simply provide additional connectivity options such as Wi-Fi or Bluetooth. If you can imagine something that you'd like to plug into Arduino, someone somewhere probably has it for sale.

The same goes for the Raspberry Pi, with everything from breakout boards for simple circuit connections to camera kits that are designed specifically with the Pi in mind, available for purchase from websites such as Adafruit and SparkFun. You can purchase kits that will turn your Raspberry Pi into anonymity proxies and remote Wi-Fi cameras, and more and more connectors and kits are available almost daily. You can, of course, even buy a card that connects the Arduino to the Raspberry Pi, cleverly called the A La Mode (www.makershed.com/AlaMode_for _Raspberry_Pi_p/mkwy1.htm).

These are only the tip of the iceberg for open hardware, as different boards are released constantly. Specialized or improved versions of these boards, such as the BeagleBone board (http://beagleboard.org/), allow for more focused or particular development and use. Arduino boards are getting smaller and cheaper, with some available for under ten dollars and smaller than a quarter.

When you combine these hardware pieces with the ability to custom print cases/containers for them with increasingly inexpensive 3-D printing technology, you have bespoke manufacturing at an individual library level. Use the recipe to plug A into B, and you have a working project; then search Thingiverse for a case/container or design one yourself. Print it out on your 3-D printer, and you've got a solution for a problem that is just as good—and better in many ways—than the custom hardware you're buying from a vendor.

IMPLEMENTATION

How does this fit into a library context? What sorts of problems could this solve? One thing that all libraries should be collecting is basic statistics, such as gate/door count. Showing that your building is busy is a natural and honest statistic to report to the agencies that hold the funding strings for libraries, whether it be the provost at a university or the board of a public library. It is a basic statistic, a foundation against which other statistics such as circulation can be compared and discussed. And while most libraries aren't buying gate/people counters yearly, I bet that between servicing and purchase price, libraries spend hundreds of dollars per year—and in some cases, thousands—on just this single piece of reasonably simple hardware.

All it will take is one library or librarian writing the code for a gate counter (and not even writing, just adapting existing code) and releasing it freely online, and the cost for implementing a system could plummet to just the cost of the basic hardware and a few minutes of time. As very rough math, a gate counter from a typical library vendor costs $300 and up, to as much as thousands for one with wireless capabilities. For well under $100 worth of hardware, a library could build a gate counter that is more fully featured—and certainly better understood and repairable—than the existing options.

Not only that, but once the cost of hardware hits a certain point (as it has with sensors), it becomes trivial to measure things that almost no one measures currently. Once the cost of the hardware for one of these gate counters drops to $50, it is suddenly very tempting to sprinkle them liberally throughout a library. How would you change your usage policies if you could look at minute-to-minute occupancy numbers for your study rooms? Using counters around the library would give you a much more robust understanding of room usage and traffic patterns, and would give you data to better the experience of your patrons.

The exciting thing about this isn't the data that you can measure. As William Gibson once said, "The street finds its own uses for things."[2] Once this type of inexpensive hardware is in the world, the sorts of things that it might be used to gather about are innumerable. And gate counters are only the first step of sensors that could be used. Want to see if occupancy actually correlates with noise levels, or is there really some other reason you get noise complaints only on certain nights? Build something that will give you the data to figure it out. Build the things that measure the future.

Libraries use lots of other obvious bits of hardware that could be replaced with open hardware alternatives. Temperature and humidity sensors are another common hardware bit that libraries use, that are priced far higher than the component parts, and that could be built and replaced several times over and still save the library money over the traditional vendor. Moreover, the devices could be precisely customized. For instance, with a Raspberry Pi and a few sensors, you could have a device that e-mails you if it senses water on the ground. With a web connection, you could easily have a sensor that alerts you via Twitter when your server room is getting too hot, or that posts to Facebook when your study rooms have available spaces for the day. Much of this sort of automated interaction with the world can be offloaded to inexpensive hardware that we build ourselves.

These inexpensive boards and sensors are now on the way to enabling the quantification of just about every aspect of one's personal life. From steps taken to bites eaten, what you do every day can now be measured, recorded, analyzed, and shared in order to help you change your habits. I think this same effort—which has long been the realm of high-end retailers due to the costs involved—is now available to anyone who wants it. And I think that libraries *should* want it, very much. As we move forward into the increasingly digital future, measuring how people are using our physical spaces—and thus what we can do to ensure that they are being used effectively—will be important for us to be able to communicate to stakeholders.

This type of hardware creation can also enhance other aspects of library processes. With a small computer like the Raspberry Pi and a Microsoft Kinect (the Kinect is just a fancy pair of webcams with some sensors embedded), you could set up a small system that "watches" a set of shelves and records everything about patron browsing on those shelves. For instance, you could have such a system watch your "New Books" area and record the most popular genres that are looked at and picked up, but maybe not necessarily circulated. How many people visit that particular shelf per day? How long do they browse? What catches their eye? Systems such as this are being used in retail now, in drugstores and department stores, in order to better arrange products to catch the eye of the consumer. Libraries should be using the same types of technologies to boost their services and content, and we could do so for much lower cost with open hardware and software.

We are firmly living in the world of big data at this point. I think that George Dyson had it right when he said, "Big data is what happened when the cost of storing information became less than the cost of making the decision to throw it away."[3] Most librarians should be familiar with the phrase, and some have started talking about how we use our own big data (see, for instance, Carl Grant's blog post on moving from being reactive to proactive with data usage.[4] We are starting to have the data on hand about our virtual usage via cloud services that allow us to do really interesting things with data, as Grant points out. My suggestion vis à vis open hardware is that we need to be thinking about how we can get that same level of data from our physical spaces.

HARDWARE CAN BE FUN

We often talk in terms of outcomes and assessment of services, but rarely is the goal just to have fun—something that gets overlooked or maybe just underappreciated when talking about library services. Giving our patrons happiness, providing them with services that delight as well as inform, should be a thing that we aim for in libraries. Reading is informative, yes, and important and powerful, and libraries have been appropriately revered for their role in assisting with it. But it is also at times overwhelmingly fun and joyous. How can we make our physical spaces reflect this fun?

One possibility is to work to delight your patrons by building hardware that adds play and fun to the environment. With open hardware, it is easy to add interactivity to spaces through a huge variety of inputs and outputs. Furniture that reacts to noise levels, or digital art that reacts to sensors placed around the room, objects that react to you when you put them in the right or wrong order; just making the physical space aware of the people in it has some amazing power to direct the way that people feel about it. Using the amazing creative tools that some libraries now have at their fingertips can fundamentally change the way that people interact with our spaces, and to do so by measuring existing behaviors and then iterating to alter those behaviors is a future for libraries that I'd like to see.

I want to see libraries that understand their physical spaces as closely as they understand their collections. I want to see ambient sensors that measure the way those collections actually get used in the spaces, by the patrons. And most of all, I want to see how all this can come together to create more effective and efficient libraries.

CONCLUSION

Moore's law tells us that electronics are never again going to be as expensive or as slow as they are right at the moment you read this, no matter when you read this. The march into the future is relentless for electronics, and while it may slow sometime, I'm betting it won't in any of our lifetimes. This constant improvement and cost cutting is unique among consumer goods, where most goods get worse in quality but cheaper, or more expensive and better. To get cheaper and better all at the same time is a hard thing for humans to plan for; for this reason, it's a situation that we almost never see.

Open source software had its tipping point when the Internet emerged and suddenly reduced the cost of communication to nearly zero. Open hardware is going to have its moment as the cost of the silicon itself drives to near-but-never-exactly zero. As price decreases, the literal cost of failure does as well, providing the ability to experiment without incurring a serious budgetary setback. Just a few years ago, if you wanted to have a piece of custom hardware, it would have cost you tens of thousands of dollars just to start the process of production. Now you can design, build, and even house your electronics project for less than the cost of a tank of gas in many cases. As the price continues to drop (as it assuredly will), implementation and use of these technologies becomes more and more tempting, until at some point in the future it will be trivial to produce working hardware models of things that help you day to day.

Libraries need to be considering this transition from "hardware is difficult and expensive" to "hardware is cheap and trivial." Libraries are rarely the early movers in technology. Looking back over the last couple of decades, we were late to the party on open source, late to the party on mobile, and, I would say as I write this, we are late to the party on social technologies. The measurement and quantification of everything that happens is coming, and unless we are very careful, it will be a space that is overwhelmed by private companies and locked off for open experimentation. Building our own hardware, working to make the things that measure our future, is as important as all the technological innovations that I listed above. Let's not be late to this party.

NOTES

1. I am using *makerspace* as a catchall term for "creation spaces," which in some libraries are called fablabs or tinkerspaces.

2. William Gibson, "Burning Chrome," *Omni*, July 1982, 72–77.

3. Tim O'Reilly, "George Dyson's Definition of 'Big Data,'" Google+ post, May 6, 2013, https://plus.google.com/+TimOReilly/posts/Ej72QmgdJTf.

4. Carl Grant, "The Approaching Divide in the Provision of Library Services," *Thoughts from Carl Grant* (blog), August 21, 2013, http://thoughts.care-affiliates.com/2013/08/the-approaching-divide-in-provision-of.html.

About the Contributors

BRIGITTE BELL holds BA and MLIS degrees from Dominican University in River Forest, Illinois. She currently serves as the instruction librarian at the University of St. Francis in Joliet, Illinois. Bell is responsible for providing bibliographic instruction to students at the undergraduate, graduate, and doctoral levels. Her special interests include academic technology and information literacy advocacy/assessment. Bell can be contacted via e-mail at bbell@stfrancis.edu.

STEVEN K. BOWERS is the director of the Detroit Area Library Network (DALNET), at Wayne State University. As director of DALNET, Bowers is responsible for administration of the consortium, oversight of project management, and development of online services. He previously worked as a systems librarian. Bowers teaches a course on integrated library systems for the Wayne State University School of Library and Information Science, his alma mater, and he presents annually at state and national conferences. Bowers was featured in the 2008 edition of *Library Journal*'s Movers & Shakers for his work integrating Web 2.0 features into online library catalogs. He can be reached at steven.bowers@wayne.edu.

TERRY COTTRELL is dean of Academic Technology and Library Services at the University of St. Francis in Joliet, Illinois. Cottrell has previously served on the Illinois Library Association, RAILS, and CARLI executive boards, as well as the Plainfield (Illinois) Public Library board of trustees. He holds BA and MBA degrees from the University of St. Francis and an MSLIS degree from the University of Illinois–Urbana-Champaign. Cottrell is a doctoral candidate in instructional technology at Northern Illinois University in DeKalb. He can be contacted at tcottrell@stfrancis.edu.

WILLIAM DENTON is web librarian at York University. His work centers on the library's web presence: what the site looks like, what it offers, how people use it, and how other librarians can do more anywhere on the Web. He completed his master of information studies in 2005. Before that, he worked for a decade as a web developer and programmer. His research is on information visualization and augmented reality. His web site is www.miskatonic.org; he can be reached at wdenton@yorku.ca.

JASON GRIFFEY is associate professor and chief technology strategist for the library at the University of Tennessee at Chattanooga. His latest book is *Mobile Technology and Libraries* (ALA Editions 2010), and he has written multiple library technology reports for the American Library Association. Griffey was named a *Library Journal* Mover & Shaker in 2009 and speaks internationally on the future of libraries, mobile technology, e-books, and other technology-related issues. His latest obsession is the LibraryBox Project (librarybox.us), a portable digital file distribution system. He can be followed at www.jasongriffey.net, and spends his free time with his daughter Eliza and preparing for the inevitable zombie uprising.

DEVIN HIGGINS is a Digital Library programmer and part-time Digital Humanities librarian at Michigan State University. His current professional interests include text mining, data visualization, and building digital collections that promote user exploration. He can be reached at higgi135@msu.edu.

A. J. MILLION teaches digital media and Web development courses to library students and educators at the University of Missouri. His interests connect the use of information technology by public institutions to the process of adaptation and broader conceptions of the common good. He may be reached at ajmillion@gmail.com.

DAVID MOODY is currently the web master of the University of Virginia Medical Library and president of AuthorsPress Publishing. David is a veteran of the U.S. Navy, with a bachelor's degree in nuclear engineering. He left the nuclear engineering field after fourteen years for a second career in information technology, started four Internet companies, and eventually became a founding member of the University of Virginia Hospital Web Development Center. He has been working in the Internet development industry for thirteen years. Moody enjoys snowboarding and a good glass of Virginia wine, but not at the same time. He can be reached at dam8u@virginia.edu.

HEATHER LEA MOULAISON is an assistant professor at the University of Missouri's iSchool, where she teaches classes in organization of information (including cataloging and metadata) and on emerging technologies. Her primary research area falls at the intersection of new technologies and the organizing of information with an emphasis on the use of digital library systems. Moulaison is coauthor of *Digital Preservation for Libraries, Archives, and Museums* (Scarecrow Press, 2014) with E. M. Corrado and has presented nationally and internationally on topics relating to libraries and technology.

V. P. NAGRAJ is relatively new to the field of web development. His degree from the University of Virginia is in English. Approaching the world of web design from the trenches of the library circulation desk has allowed him to build better user interfaces that reflect the day-to-day needs of librarians. He can be reached at vpn7n@virginia.edu.

ANSON PARKER is an application developer at the University of Virginia's Claude Moore Health Sciences Library. He can be reached at adp6j@virginia.edu.

ELLIOT J. POLAK joined Wayne State University in 2012 and is currently the coordinator for Discovery Services, responsible for providing strategic direction for library discovery through technology development and project management for University Libraries. Prior to joining Wayne State, Polak spent three years at Norwich University serving as the head of Library Technology, responsible for evaluating, maintaining, and implementing systems at Kreitzberg Library. Polak graduated from University of Wisconsin–Madison with an MA in library and information studies, and holds a BS in information systems from California State University–Northridge. He can be reached at elliot.polak@wayne.edu.

KENNETH J. VARNUM is the Web Systems manager at the University of Michigan Library, where he manages the library website and development of new features and functionality. He received a master's degree from the University of Michigan's School of Information and a bachelor of arts from Grinnell College. He has worked in a range of library settings—large and small academic, corporate, and special. He led the University of Michigan's implementation of Summon using the Summon API in a Drupal site in 2010. An active member of the library technology world for nineteen years, Varnum's research and professional interests range from Drupal and site redesign to user-generated content. ALA TechSource published his first book, *Drupal in Libraries*, in 2012.

JEREMY YORK is the assistant director of HathiTrust. He began working for HathiTrust a few months before it was formally launched in 2008. His primary duties include coordination of HathiTrust projects and initiatives related to repository administration, communications, user support, and other operational activities. York received a bachelor's degree in history from Emory University and a master of information science from the University of Michigan, with a specialization in archives and records management. He can be reached at jjyork@umich.edu.

Index

Note: page numbers for tables and figures are in italics.

technology
    competition and, 6–8
    definition of, 5
    obsolete, 6
text analysis, 85, 89–92
Text Encoding Initiative (TEI), 89–90
text mining
    future of, 93–97
    library connections and, 89–93
    overview of, 85–86
    in practice, 87–89
    usage of, 86–87
textual analysis tools, 88–89
3D Compass+, *20*
3-D printers, 118
topic modeling, 92–93
trust, 111–112
Trustworthy Digital Repositories, 103

U
Underwood, Ted, 86
Unity 3D game engine, 34
usability, 89, 91, 108
usage statistics, 51, 81, 82
user services, 107–110

V
values of librarianship, 1, 2
Vinge, Vernor, 29, 31
Voyant Tools, 89
Vuforia, 34–35
Vuzix, 35

W
web services
    creation of, 75–76
    definition of, 69
    formats for, 70
    implementation of, 82–83
    move toward, 67–68
    standards for, 70
Wikitude, 32, 33, 34, 35
WolfWalk, 17–18
Word Lens, 33
word-frequency distributions, 92

X
XML (extensible markup language), 69